ILLUSTRATED GUIDE to
KNIVES

ILLUSTRATED GUIDE to
KNIVES

Jan Suermondt

Grange
BOOKS

Published 2004 by Grange Books
an imprint of Grange Books PLC.
The Grange
Kings North Industrial Estate
Hoo nr. Rochester
Kent, UK
ME3 9ND

www.grangebooks.co.uk

All enquiries please email info@grangebooks.co.uk

All notations of errors or omissions (author inquiries, permissions) concerning the content of this
book should be addressed to:
TAJ Books 27, Ferndown Gardens, Cobham, Surrey, UK, KT11 2BH, info@tajbooks.com.

ISBN 1-84013-694-4

Printed in China.

1 2 3 4 5 08 07 06 05 04

INTRODUCTION

Knives are basic to civilization: before there was metal there were knives. All over the world Neolithic man created stone knives: the apogee of Stone Age technology being the remarkable use of flints. As ancient tools go, flints were probably the most effective; when professionally knapped, forming weapons with which man could catch, killing and butcher his prey.

As the Bronze Age took over from Stone and the Iron Age followed, blade technology improved: knives were carried by all and were used for every conceivable purpose — including fighting. After the fist, the knife is one of the most basic weapons for armed combat and one of the most effective. Every civilization has used edged weapons both for aggression and practicality — from the Ghurka kukri to the Bowie knife. Today's knives are simply the current versions of a tool with a long history and a multiplicity of forms. This book looks at the best knives available today for all their many uses.

A good knife is the most essential piece of kit any soldier or survivalist can carry and it will save lives as readily as dispatch them. By using a knife a person can hunt and kill food, cut and collect herbage, build a fire, cook; make camp, build shelter and protect themselves from close-quarter aggressors. It is truly a multi-purpose tool and intelligently used is invaluable. Soldiers carry knives for all these purposes and many more. Inevitably preferences emerge — concerning the feel and weight, quality of the blade and handle — a good knife becomes so much more than just a tool, it is a way of life. The tool needs to fit its intended purpose, whether it be for skinning a rabbit, for general survival purposes while climbing and camping, or for intended combat. Choice of knife becomes critical.

Anyone trekking and carrying all their goods needs a suitable, adaptable knife: one that is too small could prove as good as useless, while a knife that it too big can be heavy and cumbersome and more trouble than its worth. The differences between apparently similar knives are often very subtle and it takes a real exponent to immediately appreciate their inherent qualities. Choice of knife is a critical one and worthy of careful consideration.

Knives have become highly specialised for combat, survival, fighting, bayonets and so on. However, all these categories can be interchangeable depending on the blade and owner.

Arc Angel

ARC ANGEL

First popularized by the Balisong Company in the early 1980's, the Butterfly knife with its revolving handles and super strong lock proved to be a very popular design. Since the early 1990's, United States Customs has forbidden the importation of all Butterfly knives under the Switch Blade Act. To fill this gap in the market Cold Steel introduced its own range of Butterfly knives under the name Arc Angel. Cold Steels Arc-Angel Butterfly knives are produced in the USA.

The blades are flat ground in Carbon V steel and the skeleton handles are CNC machined out of solid Titanium billets for maximum strength without unnecessary weight or bulkiness. Each knife is hand polished and assembled by skilled technicians. Finally to increase the portability of the Arc-Angel, Cold Steel have integrated a state of the art pocket clip.

Blade: 4 1/4"
Handle: 5 7/16"
Overall: 9 11/16"
Thick: 1/8"
Weight: 4.3oz.
Carbon V¨ Blades with Titanium handles.
Stainless Pocket/Belt Clip

Black Bear Classic

BLACK BEAR CLASSIC

First developed by Bob Loveless, one of the founding members of the knife maker's guild, the Black Bear Classic is perhaps the quintessential combat knife. Its 8" blade offers excellent reach, and the sub hilt practically eliminates the possibility of the hand being dislodged or coming into contact with the blade.

Specifications:
Blade: 8"
Handle: 5 1/2"
Overall: 13 1/2"
Thick: 3/16"
Weight: 12.7oz.
AUS 8A Stainless steel with 300 Series Stainless guards.
Black linen Micarta handles.
Leather sheath with sharpening stone and pouch

Bolo Machete

BOLO MACHETE

Known throughout Asia and Pacific Rim, the Bolo Machete features a fat point that shifts its weight forward where it can do the most good when heavy chopping or slashing is called for. It's an excellent survival tool and will open a coconut or chop down a tree with equal ease.

Weight: 17.3 oz.
Blade Thickness: 5/64"
Blade Length: 16 3/8"
Handle: 5 5/8" long. Polypropylene
Steel: 1055 Carbon Steel w/ Black Baked on Anti Rust Matte Finish
Overall Length: 22"
Sheath: Black Nylon

Double Edged Machete

Double Edged Machete

The versatile design of the Double Edged Machete makes it very adaptable in use.

Perhaps you might keep one edge thin for the light vegetation and the other a little on the thicker side for the heavy stuff. Or your may opt to keep both edges equally sharp so that when an edge gets dull after heavy use, you can flip it over and keep on going. The double edged design enables the user to cut from any angle with a turn of the wrist.

Weight: 18 oz.
Blade Thick: 1/16"
Blade Length: 16"
Handle: 6 1/2" Quarter sawn Ash
Overall: 22 1/2"
Steel: 1055 Carbon Steel w/ Black Baked on Anti Rust Matte Finish

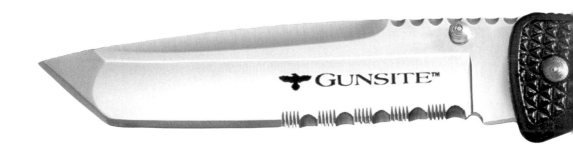

GunSite II

GUNSITE SERIES

The Gunsite Folders are the first authorized and official knives of the renowned Gunsite Training Center, one of the leading U.S. providers of training in firearms education. Intelligently styled, these Tanto folders are rugged and hard-wearing. Featuring a versatile 50/50 combination plain and serrated edge style with extraordinarily strong locking mechanisms (the larger model can withstand a strain of up to 130 pounds). The Gunsite folders have an all Zytel handle with and integral pocket clip for easy carry.

GUNSITE II
Specifications:
Blade: 4"
Handle: 5 1/8"
Overall: 9 1/8"
Thick: 1/8"
Weight: 3.5oz.
Blade: AUS 8A Steel.
Handle: Zytel

GUNSITE
Specifications:
Blade: 5"
Handle: 6"
Overall: 11"
Thick: 1/8"
Weight: 5.4oz.
Blade: AUS 8A Steel.
Handle: Zytel

Gurka Kukri

GURKHA KUKRI

The classic Kukri blade shape has developed over hundreds of years and is derived from the ancient Greek Kopis and The Roman Machaira known for their tremendous chopping cuts.

The Gurkha Kukri will out-chop any factory or handmade knives, including swords twice its size. Taking advantage of its downward curving blade and long, V shaped cross section, the Gurkha Kukri places its edge at an angle to a target, creating a powerful shearing effect. The heaviest Kukri on the market, the blade is almost an inch wider near the tip than it is at the handle, which shifts the knife's balance point forward. This allows a substantial blow to be struck with minimal effort, using inertia alone to complete the cut.

GURKHA KUKRI (Standard Leather Sheath)
Specifications:
Weight: 22 oz.
Blade Thickness: 5/16".
Blade Length: 12".
Handle: 5" long. Kraton .
Steel: Carbon V.
Overall Length: 17" .
Black Epoxy Powder Coat.
Sheath: Black Leather

GURKHA KUKRI (Concealex Sheath)
Specifications:
Weight: 22 oz.
Blade Thickness: 5/16".
Blade Length: 12".
Handle: 5" long. Kraton .
Steel: Carbon V.
Overall Length: 17" .
Black Epoxy Powder Coat.
Sheath: Concealex

Heavy Machete

HEAVY MACHETE

This is the heaviest machete in Cold Steel's range. The blade widens dramatically toward the tip for maximum cutting and chopping power. It is deal for really heavy work.

Weight: 24 oz.
Blade Thick: 5/64"
Blade Length: 14 5/8"
Handle: 5 5/8" long. Polypropylene
Steel: 1055 Carbon Steel w/ Black Baked on Anti Rust Matte Finish
Sheath: Black Nylon
Overall Length: 20 1/4"

Kukri Machete

KUKRI MACHETE

This is cold Steel's budget version of their Ghurkha and LTC machetes. It retains the highly effective Kukri blade shape, but with a lower grade of materials and finish. That said is still a good, inexpensive, workhorse model. It features the distinctive weight-forward balance of the top-of-the-line models, and always presents its edge on an angle so it's guaranteed to bite deep with every stroke. This knife is supplied with a Cordura sheath.

Weight: 16 oz.
Blade Thick: 7/64" (2.75mm)
Blade Length: 13"
Handle: 5" Polypropylene
Overall: 18"
Steel: 1055 Carbon Steel w/ Black Baked on Anti Rust Matte Finish
Sheath: Cordura Sheath

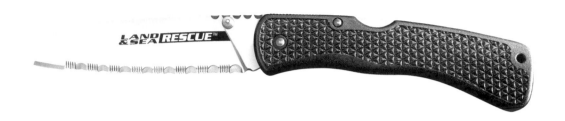

Land and Sea Rescue Knife

LAND AND SEA RESCUE KNIFE

The Land and Sea/Rescue Knife is designed for use in emergency rescue situations. It can be easily opened, and the innovative rocker lock allows worry-free deployment when a life is on the line. Once locked open, the blade can cut through a wide range of materials with its wide, flat ground surface and serrated edge. The sheeps foot shaped AUS 8A Stainless blade is ideal for rescue situations because it is less likely to injure accident victims when cutting away seat belts or clothing. And the tough, Zytel handle is contoured and deeply checkered for a solid, non-slip grip. The Land and Sea/Rescue Knife sports a small, but powerful steel pocket clip, to keep the blade within easy reach at all times.

Blade: 4"
Steel: AUS 8A Stainless
Handle: 5 1/16", Zytel handle
Overall: 9 1/16"
Thick: 1/8"
Weight: 3.5oz.
Features Steel Pocket Clip

Light Machete

LIGHT MACHETE

Cold Steel's light machete is perfect for cutting grass, weeds, vines, brush, and briars. It is widely used in Africa for harvesting corn and other crops.

Weight: 16 oz.
Blade Thick: 5/64"
Blade Length: 14 7/8"
Handle: 5 5/8" long. Polypropylene
Steel: 1055 Carbon Steel w/ Black Baked on Anti Rust Matte Finish
Sheath: Black Nylon
Overall Length: 20 1/2"

LTC Kukri

LTC KUKRI

This is Cold Steel's top of the range machete. The curve of their LTC Kukri's blade is very important because no matter what part of the blade makes contact with a target, the edge is always presented at an angle. This creates a shearing motion, so that the edge slices through the target as the weight of the blade drives it deeper. The is made out of SAE 1055 medium carbon steel and is dipped in a special antirust solution before being coated with a black baked on finish. Each machete comes with a good utility edge that will cut right out of the box and, with a little work, can be made hair shaving sharp. The handles of our machetes are made out of Kraton polypropylene and permanently injected molded around the blade's tang. They have been designed to provide a comfortable secure grip and to last practically forever, as they are highly resistant to chipping , cracking or breaking.

Blade: 12"
Overall: 17"
Thickness: 3/16"
Weight: 19.1 oz.
Steel: Carbon V
Kraton Handle

Night Force

NIGHT FORCE

The Night Force is a tactical folding knife. It has an extra wide Bowie style blade with a false edge that terminates in a sharp point. This configuration has proven to ideal for a performance knife as it will pierce or shear through most materials. The blade has a black Teflon finish to minimize light reflection and rust. Equal attention to detail has been paid to the Zytel handle of the Night Force. It is injection moulded in two parts. These parts, or halves, are then reinforced by a stainless steel liner and then bolted together. The result is a stiff, rigid handle that is extremely lightweight yet practically unbreakable. The Night Force folder features an in-house designed leaf spring lock. Extensive testing has proved this lock will reliably hold 100 lbs. or more without catastrophic failure, providing a good marginof safety. There are thumb studs on both sides of the blade for one handed opening, and an unobtrusive pocket clip on the right side of the handle.

Blade: 4"
Handle: 5"
Overall: 9"
Thick: 1/8"
Weight: 5.1oz.
440 A Stainless Sub Zero Quenched
Zytel Handle
Stainless Pocket/Belt Clip

OSS

The OSS subhilt fighter is designed to offer all the advantages and performance of a custom knife at a fraction of the price. The double edged blade is made of Carbon V steel for strength and edge retention and comes razor sharp. For the ultimate grip the handle, guard, and subhilt are injection molded in one integral piece of Kraton. This saves unnecessary costs while delivering the durability, security, and control the subhilt is famous for. To house the blade safely, yet leave it ready for instant use, every OSS comes with a high tech tactical style sheath made of Secure-Ex and Cordura.

Weight: 9 oz.
Blade Thickness: 3/16"
Blade Length: 8 1/4"
Handle: 4 3/4" long. Kraton
Steel: Carbon V
Overall Length: 13 3/8" Black Epoxy Powder Coat
Sheath: Secure-Ex

OSS

OSS

Panga Machete

Panga Machete

This is the traditional style machete on the African continent. It is excellent for cutting thick brush and chopping down saplings and small trees. It also makes a fearsome emergency weapon.

Weight: 19 oz.
Blade Thick: 5/64"
Blade Length: 16"
Handle: 5 5/8" long. Polypropylene
Steel: 1055 Carbon Steel w/ Black Baked on Anti Rust Matte Finish
Overall Length: 21 5/8"
Sheath: Black Nylon

Peace Keeper I

PEACE KEEPERS

Cold Steel's Peace Keepers double edged knives are designed to avoid the fragility sometimes associated with dagger style knives. Unlike most boot knives and daggers, the Peace Keeper's spear point offers considerable resistance to bending or breaking. Manufactured in 420 Sub Zero Quench Stainless for lower maintenance, Peace Keepers are treated with Cold Steel's custom heat treatment, to improve strength, toughness, and edge retention.

PEACE KEEPER I
Specifications:
Overall: 12 1/4"
Blade: 7"
Thickness: 3/16"
Weight: 7.9 oz.
Steel: 420 Sub Zero Quench with bead blast finish
Sheath: Secure-Ex

PEACE KEEPER II
Specifications:
Overall: 9 3/4"
Blade: 5 1/2"
Thickness: 3/16"
Weight: 5.6 oz.
Steel: 420 Sub Zero Quench with bead blast finish
Sheath: Secure-Ex

Peace Keeper II

Pro Lite Clip Point

PRO LITE FOLDERS

Made for the professional hunter, guide, or outfitter the Pro Lite folders are a range of general utility knives. Available in clip point or drop point blade styles, they're big and wide with plenty of belly and ground thin at the edge so they will sheer deep and cut cleanly into anything. The tough, 440A Sub Zero Quench blades are honed to hair shaving sharpness for an edge that will stand up to skin or scale. The handles fitted to the Pro Lites are made out of Zytel , a tough polypropolene. They're injection moulded in two parts then reinforced with stainless steel liners and locked together by five bolts. The blade is rigidly locked open with the Cold Steel designed leaf spring lock. This locking mechanism has been extensively tested and will hold 100 lbs. without catastrophic failure making it the equal of any lock in the world when it comes to safety. The Pro Lite has a blade with a thumb hole for easy, ambidextrous, one handed opening and the handle is fitted with a strong pocket clip.

PRO LITE TANTO POINT
Specifications:
Weight: 5.6 oz.
Thick: 9/64" (3.5mm)
Blade: 4"
Handle: 5 1/8" Zytel¨
Steel: 440 A Stainless
Sub Zero Quenched w/ Black Teflon Coating
Overall: 9 1/8"
Stainless Pocket/Belt Clip

PRO LITE CLIP POINT
Specifications:
Weight: 5.3 oz.
Thick: 1/8" (3mm)
Blade: 4"
Handle: 5 1/8" Zytel
Steel: 440 A Stainless
Sub Zero Quenched
Overall: 9 1/8"
Stainless Pocket/Belt Clip

Pro Lite Drop Point

Pro Lite Tanto Point

R1 Military Classic

R1 MILITARY CLASSIC

This classic WWII design has seen action in every major conflict around the globe, including Korea, Vietnam, Central America and the Persian Gulf. Cold Steel's R1 Military Classic is an exact replica of the original.

Blade: 7"
Handle: 4 5/8"
Overall: 11 5/8"
Thick: 3/16"
Weight: 9.25oz.
AUS 8A Stainless seel with 300 Series Stainless guards.
Black linen Micarta handles.
Sharpening Stone included with leather sheath

Recon I

RECON I

The Recon I has been engineered to make it as strong, durable and effective as possible. The blades are made out of 440A Sub Zero Quenched stainless steel and the handles are thick Zytel, reinforced by heat-treated steel liners and five locking bolts. To compliment the tough blade and handle, the Recon I is fitted with Cold Steel's Ultra Lock locking mechanism that virtually eliminates lock failure. As befits it's tactical mission the blade is treated with a tough black Teflon finish. This finish offers several advantages; it is highly resistant to scratches and abrasions, and improves rust resistance; it eliminates glare and light reflections which may give its user away; and it causes the blade to slip through even tough material with markedly less friction. This means the knife can cut deeper and far longer than with a non-Teflon coated blade. The Recon I is equipped with a small, ambidextrous pocket clip.

Weight: 5.6 oz.
Blade Thick: 9/64" (3.5mm)
Blade Length: 4"
Handle: 5 1/3" long. Zytel
Steel: 440 A Stainless Sub Zero Quenched
Overall Length: 9 1/3" Black Teflon Finish
Locking Mechanism: Ultra Loc with Ambidextrous Stainless Pocket Clip

Recon I

Recon I

Recon Scout

RECON SCOUT

In almost every respect, the Recon Scout is simply a 7 1/2 inch Trail Master Bowie. It offers the same steel, heat treatment, blade thickness, blade shape and handle. Outside of its shorter blade length, the most significant difference is that the Recon Scout comes with a Secure-Ex sheath instead of a leather one.

Weight: 15 oz.
Blade Thick: 5/16"
Blade Length: 7 1/2"
Handle: 5" Kraton
Overall: 12 1/2"
Steel: Carbon V
Sheath: Secure-Ex Sheath

Recon Tanto

Recon Tanto

The Recon Tanto combines classic Tanto styling, the strength of Carbon V, and a comfortable, western-style handle in a very affordable package. The Recon Tanto is redefining the standard for combat knives and is fast becoming the preferred fixed blade for SWAT teams and special military units.

Blade: 7"
Handle: 4 3/4"
Overall: 11 3/4"
Thick: 3/16"
Weight: 9oz.
Comes with a black epoxy powder coat finish

Scimitar

SCIMITAR

The Scimitar is a high impact folding leaf-spring lock like no other knife available. The Scimitar blade is hollow ground from super tough AUS 8A stainless steel honed to razor sharpness and features the famous curve of its ancient namesake. It has been painstakingly designed to facilitate the most effective cutting stroke, the draw cut. The blade also has a needle sharp point which pierces at the slightest touch. Superior engineering combines traditional appeal with the latest Western technology in the contoured Zytel and steel frame handle designed exclusively by Lynn Thompson for the Cold Steel Scimitar. The pistol grip handle allows a forward, reverse or palm reinforced grip while finger grooves, checkering, a pocket clip and pommel contribute to its ease of carry and secure grip.

SCIMITAR (BLACK)
Specifications:
Weight: 4.3 oz.
Blade Thick: 9/64" (3.5mm)
Blade Length: 4"
Handle: 5" long. Zytel®
Steel: AUS 8A Stainless Steel
Overall Length: 9" Black Teflon® Coated Blade
Sheath: Stainless Pocket/Belt Clip

SCIMITAR
Specifications:
Weight: 4.3 oz.
Blade Thick: 9/64" (3.5mm)
Blade Length: 4"
Handle: 5" long. Zytel®
Steel: AUS 8A Stainless Steel
Overall Length: 9"
Sheath: Stainless Pocket/Belt Clip

Black Scimitar

Survival Rescue Knife

SURVIVAL RESCUE KNIFE

Survival/Rescue operations demand a versatile knife able to withstand extreme abuse. The SRK was designed with this in mind. No expense was spared in steel, heat treatment, and construction. The blade has a black epoxy powder coat to help protect the Carbon V steel from the elements. The 3/16" thick blade features a strong clip point that's hand honed to a superb edge. The SRK's handle sports a single quillion finger guard and a deeply checkered grip.

Blade: 6"
Handle: 4 3/4"
Overall: 10 3/4"
Thick: 3/16"
Weight: 8.2oz.

ODA

The ODA is designed to be a less expensive version of the Military Classic. Instead of a highly polished blade, the ODA features a Black Epoxy Powder Coat and an integral Kraton guard/handle which substitutes for the Military Classic's Micarta grip and stainless guard. The deeply checkered Kraton offers an even better grip than Micarta does and is equally durable. Instead of the leather sheath and stone, the ODA comes with a high tech Secure-Ex model. Secure-Ex is far more cut resistant than leather is and won't rot, crack or warp when exposed to wet or harsh weather.

Weight: 8.7 oz.
Blade Thickness: 3/16"
Blade Length: 7"
Handle: 4 3/4" long. Kraton
Steel: Carbon V
Overall Length: 11 3/4" Black Epoxy Powder Coat
Sheath: Secure-Ex

Ti-Lite (original)

Blue Anodized Ti-Lite

Ti-Lite (Zytel Handle)

Ti-Lite

Reminiscent of 1950's styled switchblades, Cold Steel's Ti-Lite tactical folders, echo the swift lines of memorable classics. The AUS 8A Stainless steel blades feature razor sharp edges and sturdy, needle sharp points. The handles, made of forged Titanium, are available in a polished titanium, or blue anodized finish. They have been CNC milled for a visually appealing look, and for maximum strength and safety, they are fitted with full-length Titanium leaf spring locks. For ease of carrying, the Ti-Lites come equipped with a small, unobtrusive steel pocket clip.

TI-LITE (ORIG. MODEL)
Specifications:
Weight: 4.6 oz.
Blade Thick: 1/8" (3mm)
Blade Length: 4"
Handle: 4 3/4" long. Titanium
Steel: AUS 8A Stainless Steel
Overall Length: 8 3/4"
Stainless Pocket/Belt Clip

BLUE ANODIZED TI-LITE
Specifications:
Weight: 4.6 oz.
Blade Thick: 1/8" (3mm)
Blade Length: 4"
Handle: 4 3/4" long. Anodized Titanium
Steel: AUS 8A
Overall Length: 8 3/4"
Stainless Pocket/Belt Clip

TRAIL GUIDE

The Trail Guides are designed as robust general-purpose folders for camp use. They are built to be as tough, with broad, extra sturdy blades made from Carbon V Steel. To maximize cutting power, we have flat ground each blade to a shallow V cross section and honed it razor sharp so it will shear through an apple or skin a deer with equal ease. The handle was designed for hard use. It's virtually unbreakable and impervious to the weather! It's made of a glass impregnated Nylon called Valox, and checkered for a firm non-slip grip. The Trail Guides are handy to carry and easy to open in emergencies. They're equipped with a custom designed pocket clip and an ambidextrous thumb hole in the blade.

TRAIL GUIDE LARGE DROP POINT
Specifications:
Weight: 3.8 oz.
Thick: 1/10"
Blade: 3 3/4"
Handle: 5" Valox
Steel: Carbon V
Overall: 8 3/4"
Stainless Pocket/Belt Clip

TRAIL GUIDE MEDIUM DROP POINT
Specifications:
Weight: 1.9 oz.
Thick: 3/32"
Blade: 2 5/8"
Handle: 3 5/8" Valox
Steel: Carbon V
Overall : 6 1/4"
Stainless Pocket/Belt Clip

Trail Guide

Trail Guide

Triple Action Tanto Point

TRIPLE ACTION

Cold Steel's Triple Action folding knives prove that formidable power and strength in a folding knife do not require the weight of an anvil. With a convenient pocket clip, and a closed length of only 5 inches, the 3.5 ounce Triple Action Folders are very compact when folded. Cold Steel is the first to offer a high quality folder featuring AUS10A stainless steel providing superb cutting ability with the finest combination of strength and flexibility. The aircraft grade aluminium handle is roll engraved with a distinctive pattern, giving the Triple Action[a] an exceptional finished look.

AUS 10A, is a high carbon stainless made in Japan. It is supplanting AUS 8A as a favoured blade making material since it equals the older steel in strength and toughness but exceeds AUS 8A by an honest 20% in edge holding ability.

TRIPLE ACTION TANTO POINT
Specifications:
Weight: 3.6 oz.
Blade: 1/8" (3mm)
Blade Length: 4"
Handle: 5 1/8"
A-5052 High Grade Aluminium
Steel: AUS 10A Stainless
Overall: 9 1/8"
Stainless Pocket/Belt Clip

TRIPLE ACTION DOUBLE EDGE
Specifications:
Weight: 3.6 oz.
Blade: 1/8" (3mm)
Blade Length: 4"
Handle: 5 1/8"
A-5052 High Grade Aluminium
Steel: AUS 10A Stainless
Overall: 9 1/8"
Stainless Pocket/Belt Clip

Triple Action Double Edge

Ultimate Hunter

Ultimate Hunter

The Ultimate Hunter was designed, by Lloyd Pendleton, as a hunting knife that has the safety and convenience of a folding knife yet has the strength and cutting power of a fixed blade. The blade featuring Lloyd's famous drop point configuration is ideal for field dressing and skinning big game animals and is stout enough to withstand considerable abuse without snapping. It's fashioned from 4 millimetre thick AUS 8A stainless steel and flat ground to an unbelievably sharp edge that will last yet remain easy to re-sharpen.

The Ultimate Hunter is fitted with a state-of-the-art rocker lock developed by Cold Steel. The precision milled, hand fitted parts and extra thick, stiff springs will provide safety under hard use and the special heat treatment, along with other refinements, make this lock a formidably strong and reliable piece of workmanship.

Blade Length: 3 1/2"
Blade Thick: 5/32" (4 mm)
Handle: 5"
Overall length: 8 1/2"
Weight: 5.9 oz.
Steel: AUS 8A Stainless Steel

UWK

The UWK is essentially an updated version of the original SOG knives from the Vietnam era and is much cheaper than an original. The new knife follows the profile of the original very closely; the only changes made were to black epoxy powder coat the blade and to utilize an integral Kraton handle and guard. In keeping with the UWK's tactical mission, a thermo plastic sheath made of Secure-Ex with an adjustable Cordura belt loop is provided as standard.

Weight: 7.8 oz.
Blade Thickness: 3/16"
Blade Length: 6 1/2"
Handle: 4 7/8" long. Kraton
Steel: Carbon V
Overall Length: 11 3/8" Black Epoxy Powder Coat
Sheath: Secure-Ex

VAQUERO SERIES

The Vaquero Series folders all feature a distinctive Nogales clip point blade style. They are precision flat ground to form a long, shallow V shaped cross section. This is ideal for shearing through thick, fibrous materials such as manila rope, cable, hose, belts, etc. The serrated edges form a sinuous double curve. This means that whatever material is struck with the inward curving portion of the edge near the hand will automatically force the remaining curved edge entirely through. These strong, handsome folders deliver an unequalled fit and finish. They are carefully machined and fitted by hand. The deeply chequered, and ergonomically designed Zytel handles are cleverly reinforced with enough rigidity, strength, and toughness to virtually last a lifetime. Double thumb studs on each side of the razor sharp blade allow open these folders to be opened with either hand. A black stainless steel pocket clip is included.

The series is available in three sizes, the largest being the six-inch Vaquero Grande, followed by a four-inch model and the third with a three-inch blade.

VAQUERO GRANDE
Specifications:
Weight: 6.4 oz.
Blade Thick: 3.5 mm
Blade Length: 6"
Steel: AUS 8A Stainless Steel
Overall Length:13 1/4"
Zytel handle and black stainless steel pocket clip.

LARGE VAQUERO
Specifications:
Weight: 3.3 oz.
Blade Thick: 3mm
Blade Length: 4"
Steel: AUS 8A Stainless Steel
Overall Length: 9"
Zytel handle and black stainless steel pocket clip.

Large Vaquero

Medium Vaquero

Medium Clip Point Voyager

VOYAGER SERIES

Due to their lightweight and convenience, Zytel handled lock backs have gained enormous popularity over heavier, traditional lock backs and Cold Steel's Voyager Series is part of the new generation of these ultra-light knives.

The Voyager Series are made from AUS 8A Stainless Steel. They feature precision milled and hand fitted parts with extra stiff springs. This provides a lock that is safer and stronger than most traditional folders. The blades are extremely wide and ground thin at the edge for tremendous shearing potential. This thin edge allows the blade to be honed to astounding sharpness and the cutting surface is continuously curved along its entire length for the most efficient possible slicing action. The high carbon content of the stainless steel, ensures good edge retention and serrations are to Cold Steel's exclusive pattern. This offers the aggressive ripping action of serrated teeth, but with a twist. Their design features groups of very small teeth separated by wide, shallow arcs. This results in the benefits of both a plain and a serrated edge, so that the knife still cuts smoothly through almost any material.

MEDIUM CLIP POINT VOYAGER
Specifications:
Blade: 3", AUS 8A Stainless Steel
Handle: 3 7/8", Zytel handle
Overall: 6 7/8"
Thick: 3/32"
Weight: 1.8 oz.
Features Steel Pocket Clip

MEDIUM TANTO POINT VOYAGER
Specifications:
Blade: 3", AUS 8A Stainless Steel
Handle: 3 7/8", Zytel handle
Overall: 6 7/8"
Thick: 3/32"
Weight: 1.8 oz.
Features: Steel Pocket Clip

Medium Tanto Point Voyager

Large Tanto Point Voyager

Large Clip Point Voyager

Extra Large Tanto Point Voyager

Extra Large Clip Point Voyager

X2 Voyager

Colt Cobra

The Colt Cobra is one of the most advanced folders in the world. It is constructed using all precision laser cut parts with CNC machining and grinding set to the closest tolerances available in the knife industry today.

The design features a liner-locking blade, a lightweight 6061 aircraft aluminium handle with an anodized military grey finish, and a stainless steel bead blasted pocket clip. The bead blasted, 440 stainless steel blade is available in a plain or 1/2 serrated blade version that utilizes a revolutionary patent pending laser-cut serration that does not require a special tool to re-sharpen. Named after the Colt .38 special, the Cobra, first released in 1951. Some models have laser-cut serrations. This is a revolutionary serration system (patent pending) that cuts faster and more smoothly than traditional scalloped serration patterns (not recommended for cutting rope or fibrous fabric materials). LASER-CUT SERRATIONS are the only serrated designs that can be sharpened using a standard system.

Colt Cobra

Two models, A and C have laser-cut serrations. This is a revolutionary serration system that cuts faster and more smoothly than traditional scalloped serration patterns but is not recommended for cutting rope or fibrous fabric materials.

• Liner locking blade
• Anodized military grey finish
• Bead-blasted 440 stainless steel pocket clip
• Closed length 4-1/2"
• Blade length 3-3/16"
• Blade thickness 1/8"
• Blade Material 440 stainless steel
• Handle Material 6061 aircraft aluminium

COLT COMBAT COMMANDER

This patented military style tactical knife, designed for the U. S. Navy's Seal Team, is constructed of one piece of tool quality, 440, stainless steel and coated with black Teflon. The skeletal design features lashing holes, finger contours, lanyard hole, non-slip thumb notches, and a wire breaker notch. A unique serrated edge cut into the blade back features a regular sharp flat design making individual sharpening of serrations unnecessary. Measures 8-7/8" overall with a 4-3/8" blade. There is heavy-duty black reinforced nylon.

Type   Fixed
Blade   Tactical Skeleton Serrations on Blade Back
Origin   Taiwan
Overall Length   8-7/8"
Blade Length   4-3/8"
Handle Length   4-1/2"
Weight   7.4 oz.
Handle   440 stainless
Blade Steel   440 stainless
Sheath   Black Nylon

COLT JUNGLE COMMANDER

This military style Machete was originally designed for the U. S. Navy's elite Seal Team. Constructed of Teflon coated, 440, stainless steel, the blade features all the weight and chopping power of a full size machete, but is more compact and easy to carry. The impact-resistant handle is constructed of black non-slip Kraton. Includes a black reinforced nylon sheath with a protective liner, storage pockets and 12" of nylon emergency cord. Sheath can also be fitted with standard military Alice clips (not included).

Overall length is 14-11/16" with a 9-3/8" blade of 440 stainless with a non-glare, black Teflon coated finish. Blade thickness is 3/16". Weighs 7.2 oz. Black nylon sheath. Made in Taiwan.

Type	Fixed
Blade	Drop Point Machete
Tang	Full
Origin	Taiwan
Overall Length	14-11/16"
Blade Length	9-3/8"
Handle Length	5-1/4"
Weight	7.2 oz.
Handle	Black Non-Slip Kraton
Blade Steel	440 Stainless
Sheath	Black Reinforced Nylon

COLT PATHFINDERS

CT 26 Colt Pathfinder - Tactical

Overall length: 12-7/8"
Blade length: 8"
Blade thickness: 1/4"
Blade material: 420 J2 stainless steel.
Handle material: Lightweight aluminium with black stainless steel hex screws, a hard coat finish and rubber inserts. Half tang.
Sheath: Impact resistant with 48" of black nylon cord. A military style lensatic compass with a glow-in-the-dark face, sight posts, brass bezel, and map wire in a hard plastic case. Includes a detachable nylon pouch.

CT 27 Colt Pathfinder - Campmate

Overall length: 12-7/8"
Blade length: 8"
Blade thickness: 1/4"
Blade material: 420 J2 stainless steel.
Handle material: Lightweight aluminium with black stainless steel hex screws, a hard coat finish and rubber inserts. Half tang.

Sheath: Impact resistant sheath with multiple grommets and belt slots for a variety of fastening options and 12' of black nylon cord.

COLT POCKET RESCUE TOOLS

These lightweight aluminium Pocket Rescue Tools are designed and developed for easy carrying. All Pocket Rescue Tools are equipped with a 1/2 serrated, 440 stainless steel blade with a non-glare bead blasted finish, a carbide glass breaker, a seat belt cutter and an extra large thumb stud & blade release mechanism for easy knife handling when the user wears gloves. These Colt products are professional knives intended for hard field use.

Colt Police Rescue Tool with Seatbelt Cutter and Glass Punch

Professional police knives intended for hard field use. The extra large thumb stud & blade release mechanism is designed for easy knife handling when the user wears gloves.

The blade is a 1/2 serrated, 440 stainless steel blade with a non-glare bead blasted finish made from bead blasted 440 stainless steel. The handle material is aluminium, anodized finish, inserts, bead blasted with a stainless steel pocket clip.
• Integrated seatbelt cutter
• Carbide glass beaker in handle
• Closed Length 4-13/16"
• Blade Length 3-5/16"
• Blade Thickness 1/8"

CT2 Colt Trailblazer

KNIFE/AXE COMBO:
The perfect companion for the hunting, camping, or outdoors enthusiast. This unique axe features a companion knife that is carried inside the axe handle. A built-in spring mechanism releases the knife with a simple push of a button. The axe features a high tech nylon handle that is reinforced with fibreglass to provide superior strength and impact resistance.

AXE:
Overall length: 12-3/8"
Axe head material: High Carbon Tool Steel
Handle material: 3% Fibreglass reinforced nylon with a chequered grip and rampant Colt logo moulded into the side.

KNIFE:
Overall length: 8"
Blade length: 4"
Blade thickness: 1/8"
Blade material: 420 J2 stainless steel
Handle material: Black rubber with a chequered grip, stainless steel guard, and black cast metal pommel.

14K Summit

The 14K Summit series knives are designed for serious climbing use.
They utilize InterFrame locking liner construction in an easily cleaned open build knife, with nickel chrome plated zinc alloy scales featuring an aircraft-style drilled skeleton design. Weight is reduced without compromising the exceptional strength. The dual liners are 420J2 stainless steel. Handles are designed with an extended guard, generous size and bead-blast finish to give improved grip. Friction grooves at the lock and on the blade spine also improve grip in wet and icy conditions.
The high-carbon, AUS 6M stainless steel blades feature a rugged modified drop point shape and bead blast finish. Blade grinds are engineered to retain maximum thickness at the tip and through the length of the spine to maximise strength. Triple-Point Serrations are available on all sizes.
Integrated into the design is the patented Lake And Walker Knife Safety (LAWKS), which effectively converts a folder into a virtual fixed blade-very reassuring when you are using your knife for difficult and tiring tasks.

Blade: Overall length: 2.50" (6.4 cm)
Cutting edge: 2.19" (5.6 cm)
Thickness: 0.10" (0.25 cm)
Steel: AUS 6M, 55-57 HRC
Handle: Closed length: 3.31 " (8.4 cm)
Weight: 2.7 oz. (76 g)

14k Summit

14k Summit LAWKS

24 PKO

24K KI.S.S., P.E.C.K AND S.S.T.

These are essentially the standard KI.S.S., P.E.C.K and S.S.T. knives with 24 karat gold detailing plus two further models, the new Black Gold KI.S.S. and P.E.C.K models featuring Teflon-plated blades and handles. All five 24K models are packaged in a black enamelled metal box as a presentation set.

All the detail hardware, including the thumb stud, blade stop screw, blade pivot screw and pocket clip, are plated with 24-karat gold.

All the innovative features of the KI.S.S. (Keep It Super Simple) and P.E.C.K (Precision Engineered Compact Knife) have been retained. The folders have only two major components-blade and frame-precision fine blanked for superior fit and smooth operation. The ingenuity of the Frame Lock design is that the secure, safe and strong blade lock selves not only as part of the frame, but also as the handle itself. A thumb stud is used to one-hand open the blade, and as the blade is fully rotated open, the Frame Lock snaps crisply in behind the blade to guarantee a sound lock-up. The blade can be closed with one-hand by simply releasing the Frame Lock.

Blade: Overall length: 2.25" (5.7 cm)
Cutting edge: 2.25" (5. 7 cm)
Thickness: 0.12" (0.30 cm)
Steel: AUS 6M, 55-57 HRC
Handle: Closed length: 3.5" (8.9 cm)
Weight: 2.2 oz. (62 g)

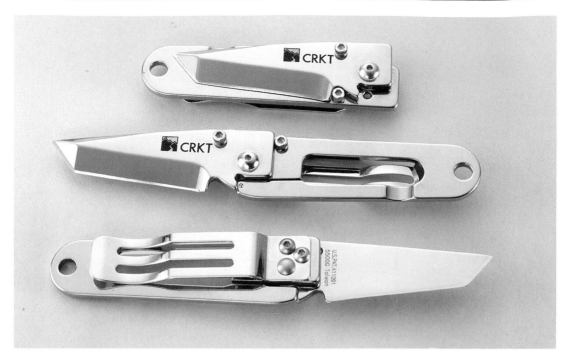

24 KKO

24 GKKO

BladeLOCK

BLADELOCK

Michael Walker, artist Craftsman, inventor of the locking liner folder, award-winning knifemaker, designer of over 20 knife-lock systems.

He says, "When I applied thumb studs to my locking liners in the '80s, it occurred to me that it could be the basis for an internal lock. I was granted the patent* for the Blade WCK" and have made many custom versions. However, no major knife manufacturer was then capable of putting the Blade WCK into production because of the challenging machining and critical tolerances required- until now." CRKT is proud that we can bring this innovation to the knife world, because it is everything you have asked for. It is an incredibly strong folding knife with a blade that locks when open, and

locks when closed. The ingenious positive lock system operates by pressing the thumb stud.

Blade: Overall length: 3.44" (8.7 cm)
Cutting edge: 3.25" (8.3 cm)
Thickness: 0.14" (0.35 cm)
Steel: AUS 6M, 55-57 HRC
Knife: Closed length: 4.50" (11.4 cm)
Weight: 4.6oz. (130 g)

BladeLOCK

BladeLOCK

Cascade LOCKBACK

CASCADE LOCKBACK

The blade is a Hammond modified clip point shape, hollow ground from AUS 6M stainless steel with a bead blast finish, and available with a Razor-Sharp or Combination Razor-Sharp and Triple-Point Serrated edge. For maximum comfort, we used our Twin-Fused™ handle technology using a rigid, injection moulded high-impact polycarbonate frame with a soft, comfortable diamond patterned injection moulded Kraton grip for a firm, safe hold. This build, combined with the rounded handle cross section, deep finger choil with guard, pronounced butt pommel and blade thumb ramp with friction grooves, results in one of the most secure and comfortable grips in any folder, at any price. This is a truly ambidextrous knife.

Blade: Overall length: 3.50" (8.9 cm)
Cutting edge: 3.50" (8.9 cm)
Thickness: 0.13" (0.35 cm)
Steel: AUS 6, 55-57 HRC
Handle: Closed length: 5.12" (13.0 cm)
Weight: 4.7 oz. (133 g)

Cascade LOCKBACK

Cascade LOCKBACK

Cascade Tactical

Cascade Tactical

CONVERGENCE

This knife is the convergence of three great ideas, resulting in one of the sleekest and most unusual locking liner folders ever. The shape is one that is gaining acclaim for award winning custom knife maker and Knife makers' Guild member Aaron Frederick of West liberty, Kentucky.

It is a remarkably simple classic profile, which is not marred by thumb studs or nail nicks. To open, just press and pull the blade end with the thumb or index finger, and the blade instantly pivots out and locks open.

Then we took the first opportunity to incorporate the patented RealEase lock release system invented by custom knife maker Charles Kain of Indianapolis, Indiana and Steve McCowen of Iota, Wisconsin. When pressed down and back with the thumb, this CNC machined button wedges the locking liner open. Just apply a little pressure with your right or left index finger and you have slick one hand closing. It makes releasing the liner lock a real ease. The result is a truly ambidextrous locking liner folder.

Blade: Overall length: 3.31 " (8.5 cm)
Cutting edge: 3.25" (8.3 cm)
Thickness: 0.12" (0.30 cm)
Steel: AUS 6M, 55-57 HRC
Handle: Closed length: 4.25" (10.8 cm)
Weight: 4.3 oz. (122 g)

E-Lock

E-Lock Starlight

Imagine the knife of the future: lightweight build, premium materials, a soft grey finish, CNC machined surfaces, a high tech lock, smooth one-hand action. Welcome to the future, because our new Elishewitz Starlight is a functional precision tool for today that would look at home in any star ship. Your first impression is, "How can a full size folder be so light?" It has a 3.25" (8.3 cm) blade, yet weighs only 3.0 oz. (85g). Your second question is, "How can such a minimal frame fit the hand so perfectly?" The stunning visual effect of the CNC machined starburst is misleading, because this is not eye candy, but a knife that is ready to get to work.

The credit goes to custom knife maker Allen Elishewitz, who designed the E-Lock Starlight as another spectacular way to use his breakthrough E-Lock mechanism. A stainless steel rocker bar with a powerful spring holds the blade rigidly in place, with a steel-on-steel lock-up, until you make the decision to press it and fold the blade. It is positive, secure, and remarkably simple.

Blade: Overall length: 3.25"(8.3 cm)
Cutting edge: 3.12" (7.9 cm)
Thickness: 0.12" (0.30 cm)
Steel: AUS 8, 57 -58 HRC
Handle: Closed length: 4.12" (10.4 cm)
Weight: 3.0 oz. (85g)

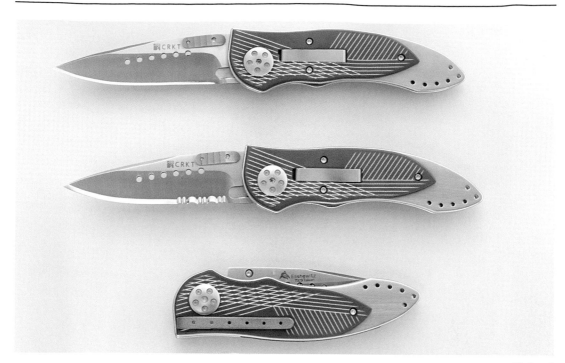

E-Lock

E-Lock

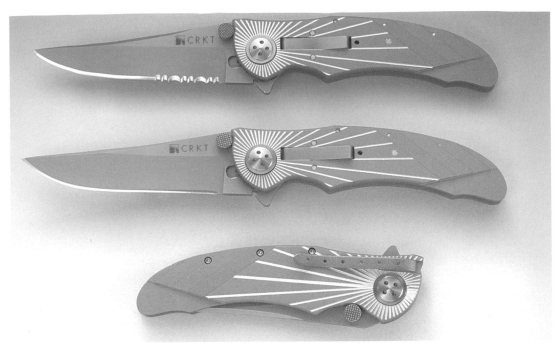

E-Lock Starlight

E-Lock Starlight

E-Lock Starlight

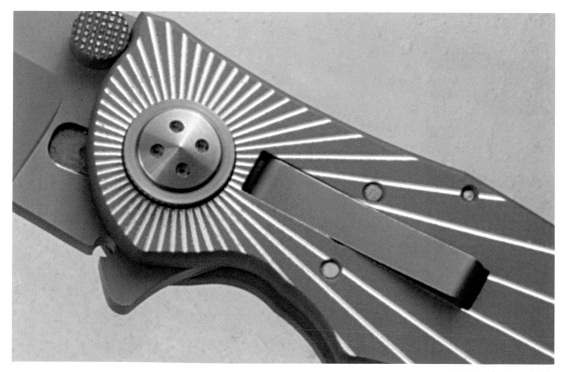

E-Lock Starlight

Carson F4

CARSON F4

The F4 is a personal work knife and is essentially, a mass-produced version of Kit Carson's custom-made F4 knife design. There are a few changes in the CRKT production version, such as a custom injection moulded Zytel Sheath, moulded contoured and textured Zytel scales, plus control friction grooves top and bottom, to make the knife comfortable and safe to use. With an overall length of just 5.5" the F 4 is still a rugged cutting tool capable of a wide variety of applications. The full tang blade is made in AUS 6M stainless steel in bead blast finish, providing a durable cutting edge. Models are available with Razor-Sharp and Combined Razor-Sharp and Triple-Point Cutting Edges. The injection moulded Zytel sheath features a 180° instantly reversible and removable pocket/gear clip, plus holes and slots, all of which allow a wide range of carry positions inside or outside of trousers, on belts, webbing, backpacks, or securely fixed to the lash tabs of personal flotation jackets.

For maximum utility, we also include a black neck chain, plus a tied black nylon lanyard fob for added effective handle length and control.

Specifications

CARSON F4
F4-02: Razor-Sharp Cutting Edge
F4-12: Combined Razor -Sharp and Triple-Point Serrated Cutting Edge
Knife: Overall length: 5.50" (14.0 cm)
Blade: Cutting edge: 2.50" (6.4 cm)
Thickness: 0.10" (0.25 cm)
Steel: AUS 6M, 55-57 HRC

F4 CONVERTIBLE SHEATH:
Material: Black Zytel
Clip: 180° reversible and removable
Length: 3.87" (9.8 cm)
Width: 1.62"(4.1 cm)
Weight: 1.4 oz. (40g)

Carson F4

Carson F4

Fixed Falcon

FIXED FALCON

The Fixed Falcon is produced in collaboration with Crawford Knives of West Memphis, Arkansas.

It is a small, utilitarian fixed-blade work knife, intended for everyday use. The knife is well balanced and offers a comfortable grip, and a wide blade that will hold an edge. It makes a perfect toolbox and workshop utility knife, in addition to being compact enough to carry as a personal tool. The full tang blade is AUS 6M stainless steel in a satin finish. The injection moulded black Zytel scales are textured for grip. Zytel was selected due to its ability to resist the oils and solvents found in workshops. The skeletal design of the Fixed Falcon not only saves weight, but the holes also offer an improved grip.

Triple-Point Serrated Cutting Edge
Knife: Overall length: 6.00" (15.2 cm)
Blade: Cutting edge: 2.12" (5.4 cm)
Thickness: 0.10" (0.25 cm)
Steel: AUS 6M, 55-57 HRC
Weight: 1.9 oz. (28 g)

Fixed Falcon

Fixed Falcon

Hammond ABC Aqua

Hammond ABC Aqua

Hammond ABC Aqua

HAMMOND ABC AQUA

The ABC Aqua was designed by Jim Hammond, a well-known custom knife maker, for use by divers and white-water rafters. The ABC (All Bases Covered) knife/sheath system incorporates a fixed-blade, general-purpose knife.

The bottom hollow ground Razor-Sharp edge is suited to fine cutting tasks. The spine incorporates a Triple-Point Serrated edge ideal for rapid rough cutting through cord, nets, fishing line, kelp, and for safe release of white-water entanglements.

The blade is a full-tang skeleton design. Manufactured in AUS 8 stainless steel, for maximum corrosion resistance, the steel is first mirror polished to close the grain, and then black titanium nitride coated. The point is blunt to prevent the knife from piercing air compartments if accidentally dropped. The ABC Aqua comes with two sets of injection molded Zytel scales, in black and high visibility yellow, both deeply textured for grip.

Blade: Cutting edge: 3.25" (8.26 cm)
Thickness: 0.16" (0.40 cm)
Steel: AUS 8, 57 -58 HRC
Knife: Overall length: 8.38" (21.3 cm)
Weight: 4.7 oz. (133 g)

Hammond ABC Operator

HAMMOND **ABC** OPERATOR

This is the land-based derivative of the ABC (All Bases Covered) diving and white-water knife/ sheath system. It retains all the characteristics of the original; fixed-blade strength, a flat profile, carry versatility, corrosion resistance, and a low reflection black finish, but married to a new blade shape. The Operator's Model has a drop point dual grind Tanto Razor-Sharp blade, a false top edge and Triple-Point Serrations. It is an ideal general-purpose fixed-blade knife for hikers, climbers, pilots, parachutists, and military personnel.

Like the ABC Aqua, the blade is a full-tang skeletal design of AUS 8 stainless steel. For maximum corrosion resistance, the steel is first mirror polished to close the grain, and then black titanium nitride coated.

Blade: Cutting edge: 3.25" (8.26 cm)
Thickness: 0.16" (0.40 cm)
Steel: AUS 8, 57 -58 HRC
Knife: Overall length: 8.38" (21.3 cm)
Weight: 4.6 oz. (130g)

Hammond Cruiser

HAMMOND CRUISER

Featured recently in Tactical Knives magazine, 1im Hammond's Cruiser is a multi-purpose folder that has garnered much praise. In Tactical Knives, Pat Covert explains, "Hammond is all about design. Using a combination of CAD (Computer Aided Design) and exhaustive research. He spends much of his time up front honing a design before ever handling the steel." This fact is obvious as you study the Cruiser, which abounds with design subtleties. For example, the handle features a forward slanted friction grooved thumb ramp and a deep finger choil for the index finger, allowing what is known as the "fencer's grip" To simplify the clean open build, a unique blade stop channel is CNC machined within the blade. This in turn, allows a friction grooved, tapered blade extension (or flipper) that aids opening the Cruiser, and then neatly completes he finger choil.

Blade: Overall length: 3.75" (9.5 cm)
Cutting edge: 3.75" (9.5 cm)
Thickness: 0.14" (0.35 cm)
Steel: AUS 6M, 55-57 HRC
Handle: Closed length: 5.25" (13.1 cm)
Weight: 6.1 oz. (173g)

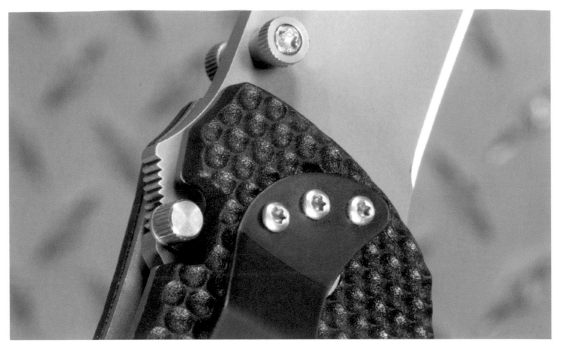

Hammond Cruiser

Hammond Cruiser

Hammond Desert Cruiser

Hammond Desert Cruiser

Hammond Desert Cruiser

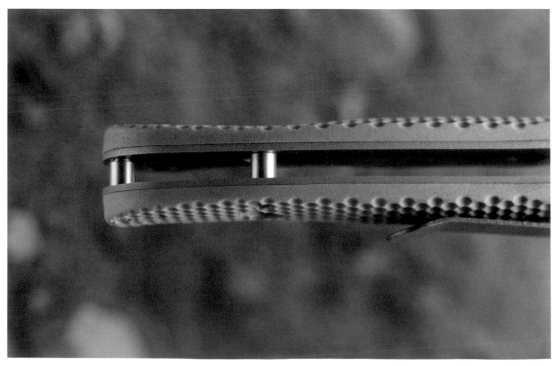

Hammond Desert Cruiser

KISS AND PECK

Not only is black the most popular colour in knives in recent years, but it also has a functional value. It is less reflective and the black coating creates a protective barrier against corrosion. This is the black-finished version of CRKT's KISS. The blade, frame and clip are treated with a special Teflon coating that is tough and long lasting.

The knife, is precision fine blanked for superior fit and smooth operation. The unique two-piece construction features an integral Frame Lock, and a design that seals the cutting edge against the handle. The blade and frame are both made of AUS 6M stainless steel. A thumb stud is used to open the blade one-handed, and as the blade is fully rotated open, the Frame Lock snaps into place behind the blade.

Blade: Overall length: 2.25" (5.7 cm)
Cutting edge: 2.25" (5.7 cm)
Thickness: 0.12" (0.30 cm)
Steel: AUS 6M, 55-57 HRC
Handle: Closed length: 3.5" (8.9 cm)
Weight: 2.2 oz. (62 g)

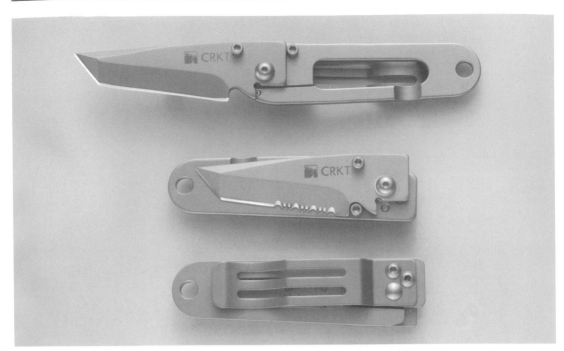

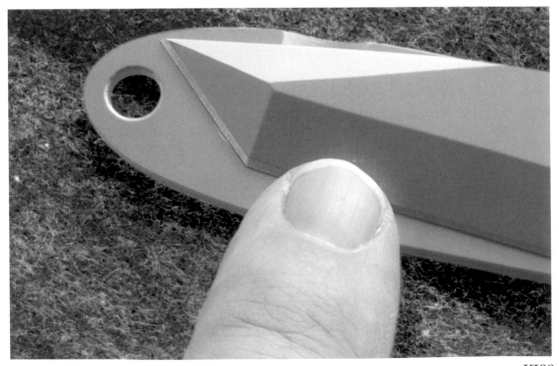

KISS

PECK

SST

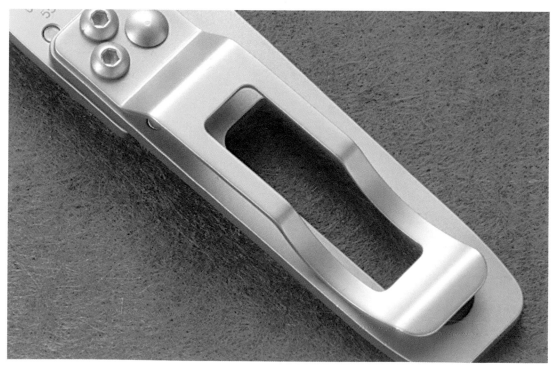

SST

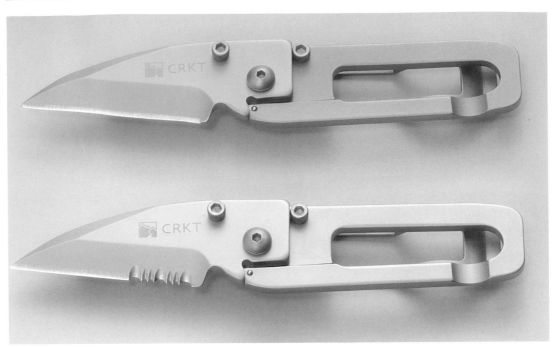

SST

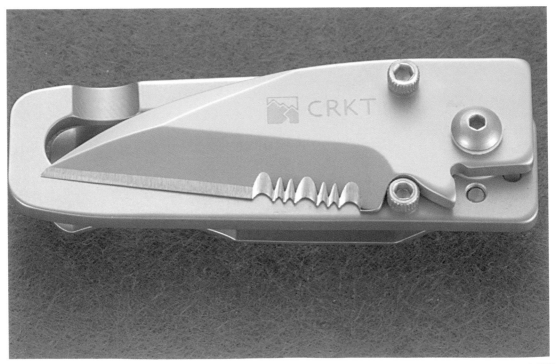

SST

Lake Signature

LAKE SIGNATURE

Ron Lake is an acknowledged master of his craft who joined the Knife makers' Guild in 1972. The Eugene, Oregon custom knife maker and author, is a member of the Cutlery Hall of Fame and has been called the father of the modem day folding knife.

CRKr is proud to present Lake's first liner lock folding knife design. It bears a strong resemblance to his interframe design known worldwide and exhibited at the Smithsonian Institution. It incorporates the most sophisticated use yet of the patented Lake And Walker Knife Safety (LAWKS), which Ron invented with Michael Walker.

Blade: Overall length: 3.25" (8.3 cm)
Cutting edge: 3.00" (7.6 cm)
Thickness: 0.12" (0.30 cm)
Steel: AUS 8, 57 -58 HRC
Handle: Closed length: 4.25" (10.8 cm)
Weight: 3.8oz. (108g)

Lake Signature

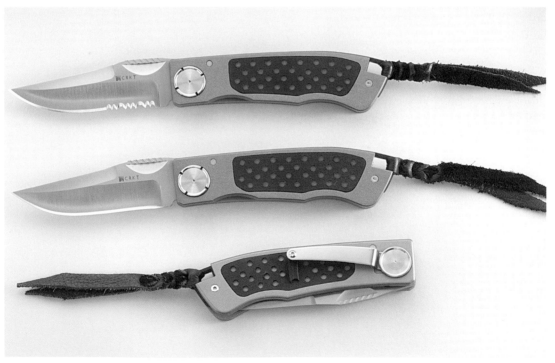

Lake Signature

Lake's Pal

LAKE'S PAL

Button locks aren't new. They have been a puzzle that kept knife makers awake at night. Typically, they have required a complex mix of liner-type springs, top spring bars and a separate pin stop. Then Ron Lake solved the riddle. His new patent pending Piston Activated Lock (PAL) has just one hardened piston that acts as a stop pin and locking and release mechanism. Study it; at first it's an enigma, then you realize it's the most user friendly folder imaginable. He says, "Normally you need three points to eliminate play, but I began to visualize how an offset shouldered piston could do the job, with the blade pivot and piston alone giving a tight lockup. I had to make several prototypes to get the offset geometry just right I thought I should call it the 'B-Damn' lock, because when I took it to the East Coast Custom Knife Show in New York, the first thing people said was usually 'I'll be damned'."

Blade: Overall length: 2.81" (7.1 cm)
Cutting edge: 2.62" (6.7 cm)
Thickness: 0.14" (0.35 cm)
Steel: AUS 8, 57 -58 HRC
Handle: Closed length: 3.75" (9.5 cm)
Weight: 4.8 oz. (136 g)

Lake's Pal

Lake's Pal

M16 Compact EDC

M16 COMPACT EDC

After the incredible success of Kit Carson's original aluminium M16'H Series, we began to get comments like this, "I love my M16 Big Dog, but I wish I had a bit more compact size that I could carry every day, both on the job and at leisure." These requests reached the point that we could not ignore them, so here they are: the M16 Compact EDC (Every Day Carry).

While we were at the task of scaling down and refining the designs, we also decided to offer models with both Black and British Racing Green handles, and with non-reflective black titanium nitride coated blades. We have made the contoured handles long enough for real work tasks. They are still 6061 T6, hard-anodized aluminium, CNC machined with a perimeter radius for comfort. A stainless steel locking liner with friction grooves gives positive locking. We also incorporated the patented Lake And Walker Knife Safety (LAWKS) into all compact M16 models, which converts them into virtual fixed blades when engaged.

Blade: Overall length: 3.06" (7.8 cm)
Cutting edge: 3.00" (7.62 cm)
Thickness: 0.08" (0.20 cm)
Steel: AUS 8, 57 -58 HRC
Handle: Closed length: 4.00" (10.2 cm)
Weight: 2.0 oz. (57g)

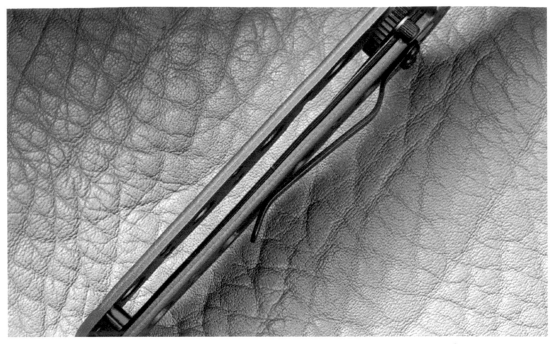

M16 Compact EDC

M16 Compact EDC

M16 Compact EDC

M16 Compact EDC

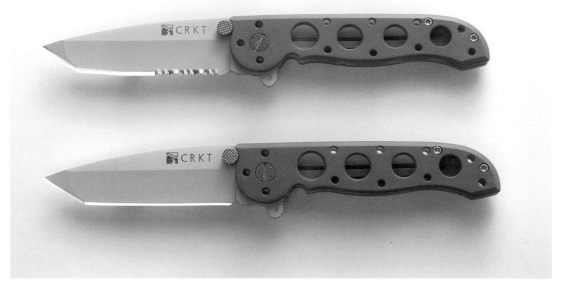

M16 Aluminium

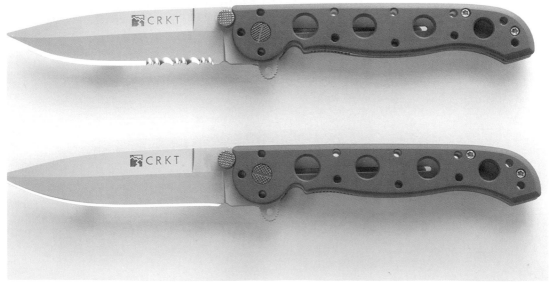

M16 Aluminium

M16 Aluminium

M16 Aluminium

M16 Carson Desert

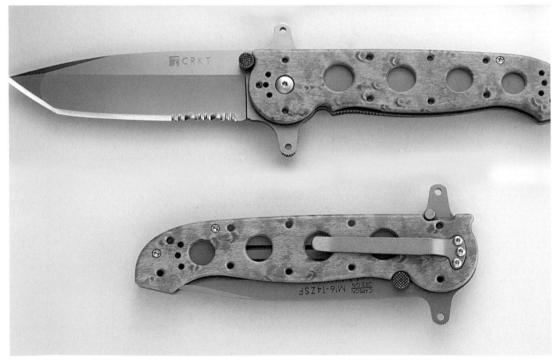

M16 Carson Desert

M16 Carson Desert

M16 Carson Desert

M16 FD

M16 FD

M16 FD

M16 FD

M16 LE

M16 LE

M16 LE

M16 LE

M16 Military

M16 Military

M16 Military

M16 Military

M16 SF

M16 SF

M16 SF

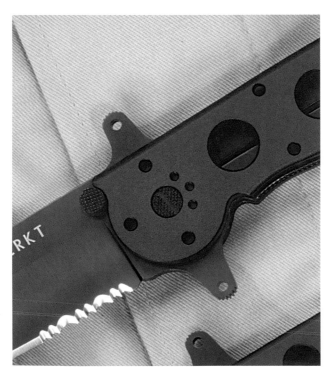

M16 SF

M16 Zytel

M16-Z

The handle is slightly heftier and wider than the M16, but it is exceptionally rigid. To some of us, it actually fills the hand better. We use our tough AUS 6M high carbon stainless steel for the blades to give greater everyday utility, and offer both Razor-Sharp and Combined Razor-Sharp and Triple-Point'" Serrated edges. All models feature the Carson Flipper, which is not only an aid to opening the blade, but acts as a positive blade guard. The M 16-02Z and 12Z are tough little bulldogs, with dual grind Tanto-style blades. The M 16-03Z and 13Z are slimmer designs with a spear point blade with false top edges. They are ideal for a variety of carry positions. The hefty M 16-04Z and 14Z Big Dogs offer larger dual grind Tanto-style blades. These are full size working knives suited to large hands and heavy-duty tasks. We've incorporated the patented * Lake And Walker Knife Safety LAWKS into all models, which converts these larger folders into virtual fixed blades when engaged.

Blade: Overall length: 3.13" (7.9 cm)
Cutting edge: 3.06" (7.8 cm)
Thickness: 0.10" (0.25 cm)
Steel: AUS 6M, 55-57 HRC
Handle: Closed length: 4.25" (10.8 cm)
Weight: 3.7oz. (105g)

M16 Zytel

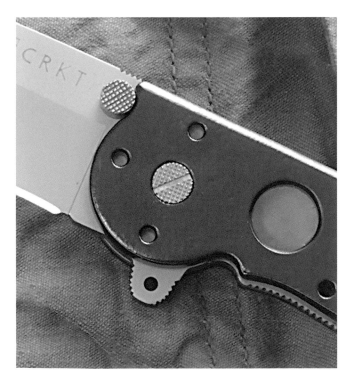

M16 Zytel

M16 Titanium

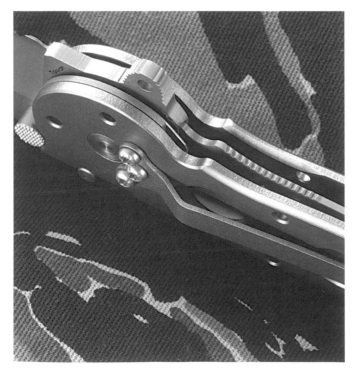

M16 Titanium

M16 Titanium

M16 Titanium

M21

M21

When a series like Kit Carson's aluminium handled line has been so successful, it is bound to spark calls for variations. In this case, the request was for a spear point blade similar to Kit's M18 design. As soon as we saw the first sketches, we new we should offer it in two sizes similar to the "Little Bulldog" and "Big Dog". The new swedged and recurved blade is ground to a spear point shape, using premium AUS 8 stainless steel in non-reflective frost finish to offer superior edge retention. The grind incorporates a false top edge and deep belly, yet retains a full width central spine for most of its width for maximum strength. We offer both Razor-sharp and Combined Razor-Sharp and Triple-Point"' Serrated edge grinds. Teflon H bearings at the blade pivot assure velvety smooth one hand opening and closing, using Kit Carson's trademark dual chequered thumb studs which also act as a blade stop. The M21 feature the very popular "Carson flipper" blade extension, which aids opening and acts as an additional blade guard.

Blade: Overall length: 3.12" (7.9 cm)
Cutting edge: 3.00" (7.6 cm)
Thickness: 0.12" (0.30 cm)
Steel: AUS 8, 57 -58 HRC
Handle: Closed length: 4.25" (10.8 cm)
Weight: 3.3 oz. (94 g)

M21

M21

F2

The Model F2 is designed for use as a fishing knife. It's deeply textured, Thermorun handle and rust resistant VG10 steel blade make it ideally suited to the purpose.

Total length	226mm	
Blade length	110mm	
Blade thickness	4.5mm	
Blade profile	Convex	
Tang	Broad	Broad
Weight	150g	
Steel	Lam VG10	
Hardness	59HRC	
Handle Material	Thermorun	
Sheath	Leather or Kydex	

F1

It took eight years to develop Model F1, a knife which today is used as a survival knife by the Swedish Air Force. The result of the extensive field tests, was an advanced, well-designed and safe knife, where strength and design go hand-in hand. The fact that it is highly popular, even on the civilian market, is of course testimony to its incredible versatility.

The combination of resilient, laminate special steel and sure grip is attractive to most. Many get on very well with this knife that over the years has become something of a signature design for Fallkniven.

Total length	210mm
Blade length	97mm
Blade thickness	4.5mm
Blade profile	Convex
Tang	Broad
Weight	150g
Steel	Lam VG10
Hardness	59HRC
Handle Material	Thermorun
Sheath	Leather or Kydex

Montana Gentleman

MONTANNA GENTLEMAN

Award winning Montana knife maker Barry Gallagher is noted for his one of-a-kind collectable art knives in exotic materials. The problem for the average knife user is that Barry is very successful, selling out his handmade custom knives quickly at the national shows, and each one goes for the price of a good used pickup. We approached Barry about producing a CRKf production folder inspired by his custom Damascus Hummingbird, featured in Blade magazine. We call the result the Montana Gentleman, a true Barry Gallagher interpretation of his classic designs that you can carry and use daily. The basic construction is our rigid InterFrame build with two 420J2 stainless steel liners, one locking. The blade is premium AUS 8 stainless steel with a Razor-Sharp edge and a Kraton filled thumb stud, pivoting smoothly on Teflon bearings at the blade pivot. We found a way to duplicate the hand file work inside and outside Barry's back spacer with CNC machining.

Blade: Overall length: 2.75" (7.0 cm)
Cutting edge: 2.50" (6.3 cm)
Thickness: 0.10" (0.25 cm)
Steel: AUS 8, 57 -58 HRC
Handle: Closed length: 3.62" (8.9 cm)
Weight: 2.5 oz. (71 g)

Montana Gentleman

Montana Gentleman

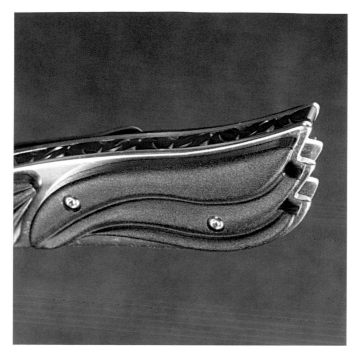

Montana Gentleman

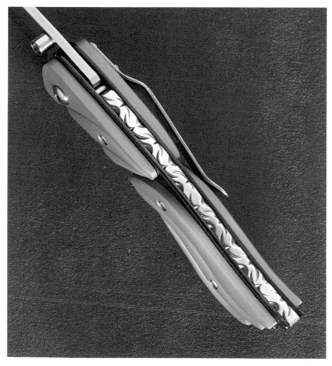

Montana Gentleman

Rollock

ROLLOCK

Since Blackie Collins invented the original Rollock in 1975, it has been an expensive cult knife that attracted an enthusiastic following. Unfortunately, production was very limited. After reaching an agreement with Rolox to manufacture the concept as a true production knife, we asked brilliant young Texas custom knife maker Allen Elishewitz to redesign the original classic. The result is a production knife that has the smoothest Rolox action ever, with an entirely new look, and a price that can put it in any pocket or purse.

Alan improved the blade shape, handle design, and added a custom stainless steel clip. To show how this sliding "folder" works, the polycarbonate scales with an engine turned pattern are translucent and we made them available in four colours.

Blade: Overall length: 2.25" (5.7 cm)
Cutting edge: 2.25" (5.7 cm)
Thickness: 0.09" (0.25cm)
Steel: AUS 6M, 55-57 HRC
Handle: Closed length: 3.50" (8.9 cm)
Weight: 2.3 oz. (65 g)

Rollock

Rollock

Rollock

Rollock

Rollock

Rollock

RSL Snap Lock

VAN HOY RSL SNAP LOCK

Ed Van Hoy is a well known North Carolina custom knife maker and instructor who has a flair for the dramatic and unusual. When his custom Snap Lock was given the Most Innovative Knife Award at the American Knife makers' Guild Show, we knew we had to offer a production version, and here it is, the Rotating Snap Lock, or RSL

Yes, there have been side-opening knives before, but none quite like Ed's. A patent is pending for his unique opening and locking mechanism. And although Ed's customs are jewellery-like in their materials and finish, we recognized that the RSL could be a very functional daily utility knife.

When closed, the AUS 6M stainless steel wishbone frame is a 100% effective blade edge guard; when open, it is a minimal but very usable handle. The harder you grip the handle, the more it locks the blade in place, thanks to twelve positive locking surfaces between the frame and locking lugs, so it is a very safe and secure system.

Blade: Overall Length: 2.56" (6.5 cm)
Cutting edge: 2.50" (6.35 cm)
Thickness: 0.12" (0.30 cm)
Steel: AUS 6M, 55-57 HRC
Handle: Closed length: 4.18" (10.3 cm)
Weight: 2.8 oz. (79 g)

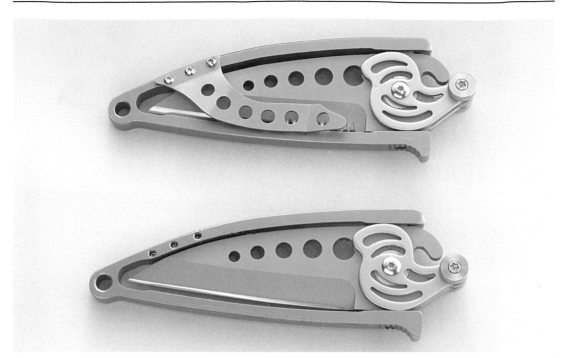

RSL Snap Lock

RSL Snap Lock

RSL Snap Lock

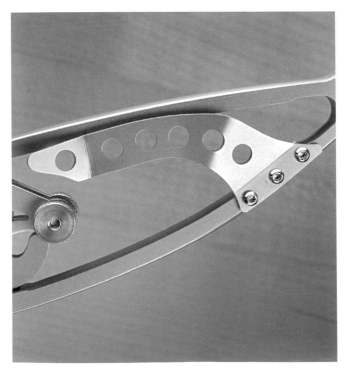

RSL Snap Lock

A1

This knife has become something of a favourite in military circles, where the requirement is for a strong, reliable and safe knife, at the same time as heavy, clumsy equipment is preferably avoided. The civilian world, naturally, has the same requirements. Despite its size, the Mod A1 is a versatile and well-balanced design. The 6 mm thick blade in laminate VG1 0 steel is very strong, and since the knife is provided with a convex edge, it cuts well even in wood. The black surface consists of Ceracoat 8H, which protects against reflections and corrosion. There is choice of a sturdy leather or a resilient Kydex sheath.

Specifications	A1	
Total length		280mm
Blade length		160mm
Blade thickness	6mm	
Blade profile	Convex	
Tang		Broad
Weight	190g	
Steel		Lam VG10
Hardness		59HRC
Handle Material	Kraton	
Sheath		Leather or Kydex

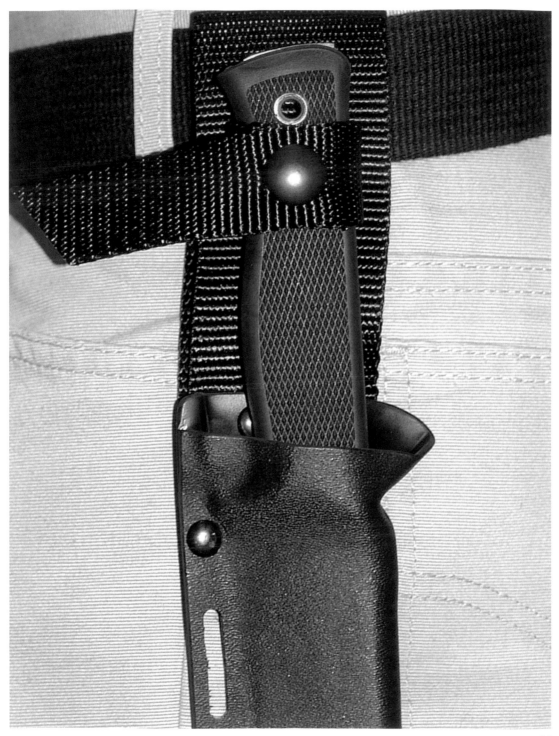

A1

A2

When you are really far from the nearest habitation, you must be able to trust your equipment. Some items must never fail, but must stand up to practically anything. Mod. A2 is an example of a strong knife that never lets you down, a knife that stands heavy use. To achieve this the blade is made of a newly developed, laminated, rust resistant steel, where the edge consists of our now famous VG10, and the sides are made from resilient 420J2 steel. The combination of these different types of steel gives a blade that both retains its edge very well and is very strong. Since the blade is ground with a convex edge, it is suitable for both cutting and chopping. There is a choice of an ox leather, or a completely weatherproof Kydex sheath.

Specifications	A2	
Total length		325mm
Blade length		202mm
Blade thickness	6mm	
Blade profile	Convex	
Tang		Broad
Weight	190g	
Steel		Lam VG10
Hardness		59HRC
Handle Material	Kraton	
Sheath	Leather or Kydex	

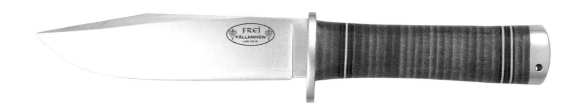

NL4 FREJ

This knife is named for Frej the god of peace in the Norse sagas, but also a god of fertility and prosperity. The Model NL4 Frej is not merely a beautiful and compact knife , but since the blade is in laminate VG10 steel, the knife is relatively strong. Frej is a slender, well-balanced knife of the highest quality, completely hand-made, like the larger models, and should last for many years.

Specifications	Frej	
Total length		244mm
Blade length		130mm
Blade thickness	5mm	
Blade profile	Convex	
Tang		Full-length
Weight	190g	
Steel		Lam VG10
Hardness		59HRC
Handle Material	Leather and Aluminium	
Finger Guard	Stainless Steel	

IDUNCX

The Model NL5cx Idun, is the standard Idun with a blade in Cowry X Damascus steel. This is probably the world's best edge steel, and definitely one of the most exclusive blades ever made. The edge comprises a powder steel with the following extreme content: C 3%, Cr 20%, Mo 1 %, V 0.3% and iron to 100%. Its hardness is no less than 64 HAC. The sides consist of stainless, 120-layer Damascus steel, and with the edge of powdered steel. The fittings are of solid nickel silver, while the rest of the handle is in stacked leather and fibre washers. The knife is manufactured in strictly limited numbers. Although an excellent utility knife, most customers acquire it for its exclusive collectability.

Specifications	Idun	
Total length		215mm
Blade length		100mm
Blade thickness	5mm	
Blade profile	Convex	
Tang		Full-length
Weight	180g	
Steel		Cowry X
Hardness		64HRC
Handle Material	Leather	
Finger Guard	Nickel Silver	
Butt		Nickel Silver

NL5 IDUN

In Norse mythology, Idun was the goddess of fertility, and responsible for guarding the apples that ensured the gods eternal youth. To many, she was also a symbol of love and rebirth. and in a poem she was referred to as the lover of the gods (asa leika). Unlike earlier models in the Northern Lights series. NL5 is a little rounder and softer in form, and therefore an excellent choice as a hunting knife. The straight, generous grip in leather gives complete control over the powerful blade in laminate VG10 steel, and makes the knife a tool as effective as it is attractive in the hands of the experienced hunter.

Specifications	Frej	
Total length		215mm
Blade length		100mm
Blade thickness	5mm	
Blade profile	Convex	
Tang		Full-length
Weight	180g	
Steel		Lam VG10
Hardness		59HRC
Handle Material	Leather	
Finger Guard	Stainless Steel	
Butt		Aluminium

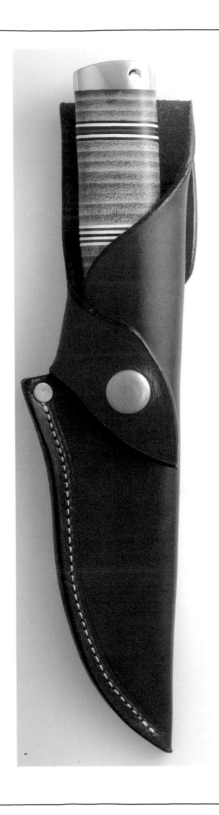

MODEL F1

Model F1

It took eight years to develop Model F1, a knife which today is used as a survival knife by the Swedish Air Force. The result of the extensive field tests, was an advanced, well-designed and safe knife, where strength and design go hand-in hand. The fact that it is highly popular, even on the civilian market, is of course testimony to its incredible versatility.

The combination of resilient, laminate special steel and sure grip is attractive to most. Many get on very well with this knife that over the years has become something of a signature design for Fallkniven.

Model F1 Green Micarta

This is another knife in Falkniven's hunting and fishing range. The tang continues through handle at full breadth, which gives the a solid weight in the hand.

Model 2

The Model F2 is designed for use as a fishing knife. It's deeply textured, Thermorun handle and rust resistant VG10 steel blade make it ideally suited to the purpose.

Specifications	F1 GM
Total length	210mm
Blade length	100mm
Blade thickness	4.5mm
Blade profile	Convex
Tang	Broad
Weight	200g
Steel	Lam VG10
Hardness	59HRC
Handle Material	Green Micarta
Thermorun	Thermorun
Sheath	Leather or Kydex

F1

F1GM

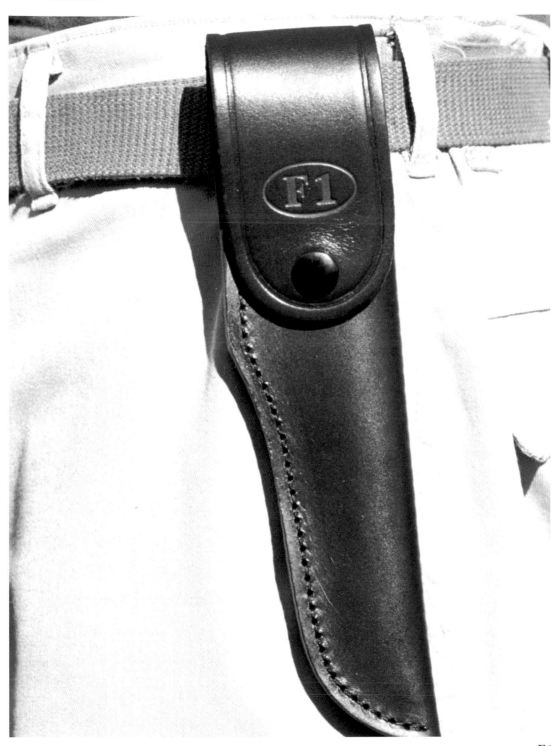

F1

Mod. G1

MOD. G1 - GARM FIGHTER

Mod. G1 is a small, sheath knife for military use. It uses an advanced special steel, VG 10, to insure strength and
good edge retention. The blade is coated in black Ceracoat 8H to avoid reflections and corrosion. The symmetrical handle in Thermorun gives the best possible grip. The knife is shipped with a Kydex plastic sheath, allowing for example for the knife to be carried round the neck, if the user prefers not to have the knife in a pocket. With a TekLok fastener (optional extra), the knife can be attached to a belt or rucksack.

Mod MC1- Modern Mine Clearance Knife
The development of Mod MC1 is the result of an official request from a NATO country, and the knife has been used in mine clearance since spring 2002.
The way the blade is ground is itself worth a little extra attention- starting with a raw piece of steel over 6mm thick, it is ground using a grind stone of a very large diameter.

This gives a slightly concave profile which is finished with convex grinding- by hand. The result is an edge which is extremely sharp, but also robust. The handle is in grip-safe Kraton, a material that is stable over time and completely resistant to solvents, and oil. The tang is the broad run-through type and is visible at the end of the handle, as is the case with many Fallkniven knives. The knife is shipped with a double locking Kydex sheath.

Total length (mm) 190 360
Blade length (mm) 90 237
Blade thickness (mm) 4,5 6
Weight (knife) 100 g 360 g
Steel VG10
Hardness 59 HAC
Handle material Thermorun Kraton
Coating CC 8H
Sheath K ydex

Mod. G1

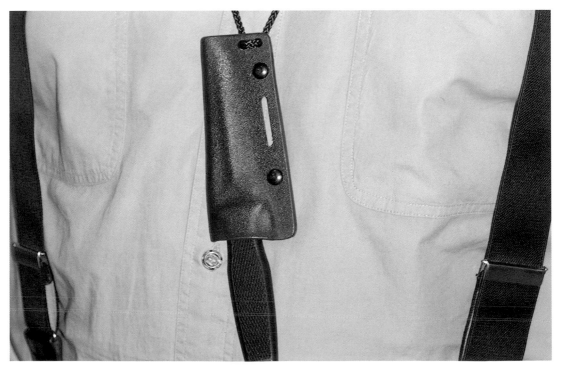

Mod. G1

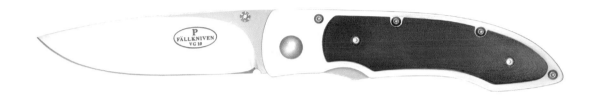

Model P

MODEL P

Fallkniven's first folding knife design, the Model P is an elegantly advanced design, and the size is evidently just right for both hunters and anglers. The knife is easy to clean, since it is open along the back. To be able to fold the blade both in and out with one hand is a detail as practical as it is smart, and the tight liner lock function feels secure. The drop point-shaped blade is manufactured in rust resistant special steel (VG10), which means that it retains its sharpness well. The knife is delivered with a black Cordura sheath that attaches to the belt.

Length folded	103mm	
Blade length		77mm
Blade thickness	3mm	
Weight	80g	
Steel		Lam VG10
Hardness		59HRC
Handle Material	420J2 Stainless Steel and Black Micarta	
Locking	Linerlock	

MODEL S1 FOREST KNIFE

The Mod. S1 is designed for scouts and mountain hikers who want the highest quality at the lowest weight. For hunting and fishing too, this knife is excellent. The blade at 13 centimetres long, has a certain chopping capability, and at five millimetre thick in specially tempered laminate VG 10 steel will withstand heavy use. The Mod S1 is the world's first stainless sheath knife with a convex-ground edge. There is a choice of an open, hinged leather sheath or a double secured all weather sheath in Kydex.

Total length		247mm
Blade length		130mm
Blade thickness	5mm	
Blade profile	Convex	
Tang		Full length
Weight	190g	
Steel		Lam VG10
Hardness		59HRC
Handle Material	Thermorun	
Sheath		Leather or Kydex

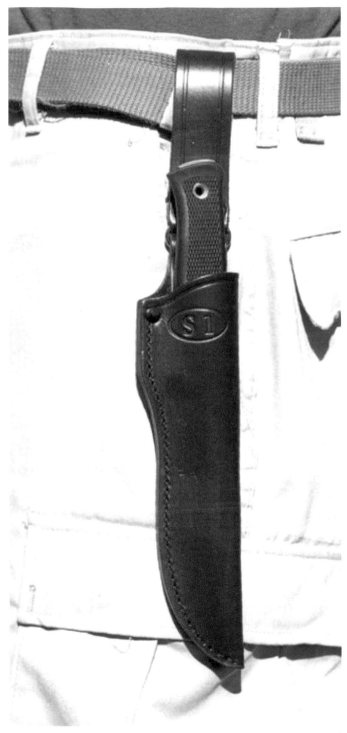

Model S1 Forest Knife

Mod. WML & H1

WM1

In most cases a 7 cm long blade is sufficient, and if in addition it is 3 mm thick and convex ground, it is both strong and sharp. Initially, this was intended as a special knife for small game hunters, but it turned out that many others were interested in this model. When it was offered with a plastic sheath that enabled the knife to be carried round the neck (or in a pocket, boot or anywhere else on the body), it was a taken up by mountain climbers, canoeists, mountain bikers, and hikers to name but a few. There is also a traditional leather sheath and a Kydex belt sheath.

H1

Although the material in this knife is high-tech, the design is from classic North Scandinavian knife making traditions. The long skinning curve, in combination with the elegantly formed tip, help to make this one of the world's best hunting knives.

The blade ridge is no less than 5 mm thick, but the edge is still sharp and stable enough to cut wood, since it is convex ground. The full handle in checked Kraton rubber gives a sure and comfortable grip. Since the knife lacks a finger guard, an advanced knife, such as Model H1 should only be used by an experienced hunter or woodsman. There is a choice of an open hinged leather sheath (with plastic inner sheath), or a weatherproof Kydex sheath.

Specifications	WM1
Total length	175mm
Blade length	71mm
Blade thickness	3.5mm
Blade profile	Convex
Tang	Broad
Weight	70g
Steel	VG10
Hardness	59HRC
Handle Material	Thermorun
Sheath	Leather or Kydex

WM1

H1

H1

NL3 NJORD

Njord was the god of fertility in the Norse sagas and was of the Vanir clan. He was also the god of sailors and fishermen, the ruler of the coasts and shores. Mod NL3 Njord is a powerful knife, well balanced and a pleasure to use. It is hard to find a better-looking all-round knife, and the strength of course lies in the laminate VG10 steel. It is a good all-round knife, stable, reliable, and beautifully made.

Total length		268mm
Blade length		150mm
Blade thickness	6mm	
Blade profile	Convex	
Tang		Full-length
Weight	280g	
Steel		Lam VG10
Hardness		59HRC
Handle Material	Leather and Aluminium	
Finger Guard	Stainless Steel	

NL3 Njord

NL2 Oden

NL2 ODEN

Named for the one-eyed Norse god, the model NL2 Oden is a powerful, versatile knife with a stainless blade in our new laminate VG1 O steel. Its chopping ability is excellent and the knife is extremely well balanced. The well-made leather handle darkens with age, acquiring a beautiful patina the more the knife is used.

Total length		323mm
Blade length		200mm
Blade thickness	6.5mm	
Blade profile	Convex	
Tang		Full-length
Weight	380g	
Steel		Lam VG10
Hardness		59HRC
Handle Material	Leather and Aluminium	
Finger Guard	Stainless Steel	

NL2 Oden

NL 1 THOR

Mod. NL1 Thor is an impressive piece which leaves no one unmoved. The blade, a massive one to say the least, in stainless laminate steel expresses raw strength, combined with fantastic bite. It is evident to all and sundry that this is an item intended solely for specialists, i.e. woodsmen with long experience of using edged implements. There is no doubting that this is a chopper to withstand heavy use; but for those who learn to handle the knife, it is also a flexible tool which can carry out practically any job one might require of a knife.

Total length		385mm
Blade length		250mm
Blade thickness	7mm	
Blade profile	Convex	
Tang		Full-length
Weight	520g	
Steel		Lam VG10
Hardness		59HRC
Handle Material	Leather and Aluminium	
Finger Guard	Stainless Steel	

NL 1 Thor

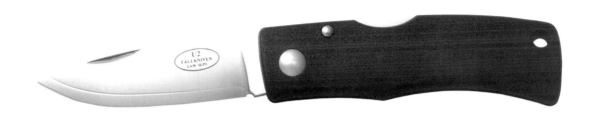

Model U2

MODEL U2

This is the world's first folding knife with a blade of laminate powder steel, the market innovation Super Gold Powder Steel, SGPS. Powder steel is extremely costly and difficult to work with, and requires advanced technology in combination with experienced knife makers. The advantage of this steel lies in its outstanding edge retention: there is simply nothing to compare today. The slim handle consists of strong composite material, which makes the knife light and pleasant to carry. With blade grooves on either side, the knife is completely symmetrical and is as easy to handle for right and left-handed users. The traditional lock back function offers no unpleasant surprises, but locks the blade in its open position with a distinct reliable click.

Length folded	86mm	
Blade length		64mm
Blade thickness	2.5mm	
Weight	42g	
Steel		SGPS
Hardness		61-62HRC
Handle Material	Zytel	
Locking	Lockback	

Model U2

Model U2

Brown Bear

BROWN BEAR

The Brown Bear Combination Set teams the heavy-duty Brown Bear Skinner/Cleaver with the Cub Bear Caping Knife and a high-quality diamond coated sharpening steel in a beautiful oiled leather sheath, for a complete hunting and field-dressing system.

The Brown Bear combo is also available in a black reinforced sheath with a D-2 tool steel serrated Cub Bear and a diamond coated sharpening steel.

Bush Camp Knife

BUSH CAMP KNIFE

The Bush Camp Knife is a large 10-1/2" long, full-tang, .16" thick knife with a 6" drop-point blade. The handles are our black rubberized Suregrip, stag or desert ironwood. The knife is designed for rugged bush camp field dressing and cooks shack duties. The blade steel is AUS 8A with a Rockwell hardness 58-59 and has the hunter's non-glare matte finish.

Cub Bear Caping Knife

CUB BEAR CAPING KNIFE

The Cub Bear Caping Knife is lightweight and designed for fine detail work. Field-tested alongside the Skinner/Cleavers in the Alaskan bush, the Cub Bear's overall length is 6-1/2" with a cutting edge of 2-3/4." This blade is ideal for the fine caping work around a trophy's eyes, ears, and nose. The deep choils in front of the handle for thumb and index finger provide excellent control for close work.

The blade is either AUS-8A stainless non-serrated or a high-carbon D-2 serrated, both with a non-glare finish. Rockwell hardness is Rc 57-59; tempering is a double-drawn, cryogenic treatment process. The Cub Bear is available with Suregrip, stag, or desert ironwood handles.

Grayling Boning Knife

GRAYLING BONING KNIFE

The Grayling Fisherman & Hunter's Boning Knife is an easily carried 10" knife with a 6" cutting edge. This knife includes a finely serrated 1" point which enables fishermen and hunters to easily cut through tough skin and sinew, and to separate muscle from large bones. The edge is hollow-ground to produce an incredibly sharp blade.

The full-tang blade is AUS-8A stainless steel and has a thicker spine than cheaper, thin fillet knives. While still slightly flexible for the fisherman, the thicker blade resists damage from bending and produces an excellent hunter's boning knife for large game. Available with black rubberized Suregrip, stag, or desert ironwood handles. The blade has a Rockwell hardness of 57-59.

HANDMADE SERIES

Knives of Alaska has a special group of knives, known as the Handmade Series. The group includes three different classic blade styles.

The first style is a classic 4-1/4" drop-point Alaskan Hunter. This knife design has been a staple for the serious hunter for decades and is renowned for its phenomenal skinning and cutting ability.

The next style is the Wolverine, a clip-point knife. This 4-1/4" long blade has a rakish point, yet maintains an effective skinning radius. This is another classic design that is probably one of the best general-purpose styles.

The final style blade is a African Hunter, a 4-1/4" partially serrated drop-point style. This knife is hollow ground, has a slightly smaller drop point than the Alaskan Hunter and is a little straighter. This knife has a truly wicked cutting edge produced by the serrations, and it is excellent for heavy cutting duties that require a sawing motion. The knife is an effective skinner due to the drop-point and smooth blade portion in front of the serrations.

All three models of a Handmade Series are individually hand-crafted from D-2 high-carbon tool steel, which is double drawn and cryogenically tempered for superior edge holding. The satin finished blades are full tang, running through the polished finger guard. The full tang feature gives all the Handmade Series models their tremendous strength. Thumb grooves on the spine of all three blade-styles provide an outstanding non-slip working surface. These knives can be ordered with a variety of handle materials, including genuine Mammoth Ivory, black Micarta, genuine stag, or desert ironwood.

Handmade Series Alaskan

Handmade Series Wolverine

HUNTER'S ULU

The "ulu" (pronounced "00-loo") is the name used to describe an ancient knife style of the north. Used by Alaskan natives for centuries, the ulu is rounded and has a long efficient cutting radius unsurpassed for skinning, fleshing, and cutting meat from the bone. Natives and many professional hunters use the knife today and prefer it for many applications over traditionally shaped knives, due to its ease of use and effectiveness. Used in combination with a traditional knife, the pair becomes unsurpassed in field-dressing tasks.

The blades are handmade from American D2 high carbon tool steel, individually hand ground, finished, and

sharpened to a hair-splitting razor edge. The heat treating process is a double draw method and then each blade is cryogenically treated so that the cutting edge is extremely sharp and stays that way even after extended use. Blades are hardened to a Rockwell of 58-60.

Choils on either side of the 2-1/4" wide blade are designed to allow the user's fingers to comfortably position themselves when using the knife. The blade is approximately .105" thick. Because each blade is individually hand ground, the thickness may vary slightly. The handle is designed to comfortably fit into the palm of the hand. Handle materials are black rubberized Suregrip, desert ironwood, G-10 Micarta, and genuine stag. The oiled leather sheath is very compact and designed to be worn on a belt.

JAEGER BONING KNIFE

Made as a premier boning and caping knife, the Jaeger is 8-1/4" overall and has a 3-1/2" cutting edge. Just under 1/8" thick (.118"), the blade steel is ATS-34, a premium grade stainless steel. The blades, treated with a cryogenic (deep freeze) and double-tempering process and at a Rockwell of 58-60, will hold an incredible edge. The non-slip ridges on the back of the blade will give you a comfortable platform on which to place either your forefinger or thumb while using the knife. Also, the individual finger grooves and deep front choil provide a comfortable and positive grip. The blade is full-tang and double-riveted, with a brass lanyard sleeve so the handle scales are securely fastened to the blade.

This is a knife that is lightweight, easy to carry, versatile and strong. The Jaeger is large enough to butcher a moose in the Alaskan bush, yet small enough to comfortably field-dress small game and fillet fish. The handle is available in either black rubberized Suregrip, desert ironwood, G-10 Micarta or genuine stag.

The sheath is made from split grain cowhide, vegetable tanned then oiled. The sheath is designed to hang at 45° off the belt. This eliminates the problems of the sheath point poking into the seat or ground.

Light Hunter

LIGHT HUNTER

The Light Hunter Mini Skinner/Cleaver is designed especially for hunters who need a powerful blade to cut through medium-size bones and perform heavy duty skinning tasks. Deer, sheep and mountain goat hunters, who hunt on extended, strenuous, high altitude expeditions, will find it to be an excellent tool that keeps the equipment weight to a minimum, yet still has enough heft to do field-dressing jobs easily and efficiently.

Each Light Hunter is handmade from, fully annealed, double-drawn and cryogenically-treated D-2 tool steel. The blade is a full 1/4" thick. There is also a large capacity gut-hook to deal with the thick hair of sheep, mountain goats, and elk . Handle materials available are black rubberized Suregrip, genuine stag or desert ironwood.

Light Hunter

Light Hunter

Muskrat

MUSKRAT

This unusually shaped knife is unbelievably effective for skinning and fleshing. The razor sharp edge extends completely along the rounded tip and top side for 1". This allows the user to skin very quickly with the knife by cutting in both directions with a quick flick of the wrist. The rounded point is also much less likely to accidentally cut through the skin of a valuable cape than is a very sharp pointed blade. This is especially important for a professional outfitter, a guide, or a hunter who wants to keep the skin or cape for tanning or mounting. The thin 1/8" thick blade is D-2 tool steel and holds an incredible edge. Total length of the full-tang knife is 6-1/2." Each knife comes with an oiled leather sheath and has black rubberized Suregrip, stag, or desert ironwood handles.

PRESENTATION SERIES

The Presentation Series is a very solidly built, stylish folder with a large selection of handles, including desert ironwood, G-10 Micarta, stag, or the incredibly beautiful and rare, genuine mammoth ivory. The knife sports a 2-1/2" VG-10 steel blade, has a Rc hardness of 59-61, and is 3-3/4" long when closed. The knife weighs 2-1/2 oz. In field tests, it completely butchered wild hogs and turkeys, and skinned a red stag and chamois in New Zealand. The two knives tested would still shave after performing these tasks. These knives are all hand-finished and individually fitted to have a perfect action. A bearing located in the liner helps provide the glass-smooth opening and closing. The bearing also engages a detent in the blade to assist in keeping the blade firmly closed until needed. As the knife is designed to be used under practical field conditions it uses an open channel construction between the liners to promote easy cleaning. It has an ample thumb stud for easy one-handed opening. This knife is available with or without a belt clip on the knife or belt clip on the sheath.

Super Cub

SUPER CUB

The Super Cub is specifically designed for executing the precise. delicate cuts so necessary for the professional guide, outfitter, hunter, fisherman. and taxidermist who demands an extremely sharp, fine pointed, durable blade for field-dressing and caping.

The Super Cub weighs only 3 oz. but is very sturdy. The knife employs a locking-liner-style lock mechanism. A ball bearing in the heat-treated stainless steel liner helps produce a smooth action as the blade is opened and closed. We also placed a detent in the rear of the blade, where the bearing will fit in the closed position to help prevent accidental opening. An "open channel" between the liners ensures easy cleaning by eliminating the block-style spacers commonly used in other folders that add weight and make them more difficult to clean. The internally threaded bushings between the liners secure the handles with eight heavy-duty Torx screws. A removable and reversible belt clip provides the user with the option to change the clip to either handle side.

Additionally, the blade's thumb stud is reversible to either side and is chamfered to fit the thumb comfortably when opening. The heat-treated and black-oxide-coated pivot and blade stop pins ensure superior wear resistance to maintain close tolerances and proper fit.

Finely chequered, rubberized Suregrip handles are very comfortable and provide a non-slip, surface whcn wet. These handles were designed specifically for use while field-dressing game. We use three separate liners to provide the necessary strength and support for the rubberized handles. We also offer models with G-I 0 micarta, desert ironwood, genuine stag, and the beautiful genuine mammoth ivory. All these materials are virtually indestructible and are well known for making attractive and durable knife handles. The blade is made in VG-10 steel and is tempered to a Rc hardness of 59-61.

The overall knife length when closed is 4-1/4", blade length is 2-5/8" and the weight is 3 oz. The serrated model has the same dimensions, with a 1" long serrated area near the handle and finger choil.

Super Cub

Super Cub

Coho Fillet Knife

COHO FILLET KNIFE

The Coho Fillet Knife, at 13" overall, is 3" longer the, smaller Grayling Fillet Knife. Designed for larger-sized fish, the Coho sports a full 8-1/2" cutting edge. Hollow ground and razor sharp, for easy filleting. The premium grade AUS-8A stainless steel blade has a Rockwell hardness of 57-59 and holds a very sharp edge. The tip is serrated to cut quickly and cleanly through the toughest fish skin and small bones.

The Coho is available in either the popular finely chequered black rubberized Suregrip, stag, or desert ironwood handles. All handles are shaped with deep finger grooves to facilitate positive gripping and comfort when cleaning fish in wet conditions. This knife comes in a lined cordura nylon sheath that will dry quicker than our traditional leather sheaths and help protect the blade.

Production Prototype Pictured

Assist I

ASSIST

Spyderco named this knife after its principal function, to assist. This version of the Assist comes with retractable carbide-tip glass breaker and snub-nosed blade.

The Assist is a lightweight folder made for emergency and fire/rescue professionals as well as for everyday use. Above the one-hand open hold sits a feature called a Cobra Hood. This is a metal cap that positions the thumb over the hole for quick opening and doubles as a textured leveraging platform for your thumb during cutting. A wavy pattern cut out of the top of the blade and again along the handle is there for controlled rope cutting. Place a rope in the groove (between the partially open blade and the handle) and squeeze the blade shut, slicing the rope in a controlled manner without an exposed cutting edge. The textured fibreglass reinforced nylon handle has a survival whistle built into the butt. A reinforced wire pocket clip screws onto either side for both left and right-handed users.

The carbide breaker is exposed when the closed knife is squeezed and retracts back in when pressure is released, keeping it out of the way until needed. This version features a snub nosed blade.

Blade Steel   VG-10
Blade Thickness   1/8in 3mm
Clip   Heavy-duty wire clip
Diameter of Blade Hole   9/16in 14mm
Edge Type   30/70
Handle Material   Fibreglass Reinforced Nylon
Hardness   59-60
Length Blade   3 11/16in 94mm
Length Closed   4 7/8in 124mm
Length Cutting Edge   3 3/16in 81mm
Length Overall   8 3/8in 214mm
Weight   4oz 115g

Production Prototype Pictured

Assist II

C28 Dragonfly

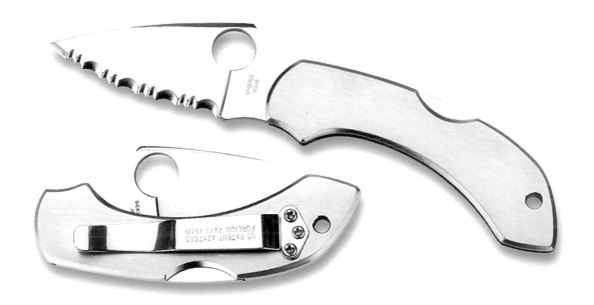

C28 DRAGONFLY

This is the slightly heavier all stainless steel Dragonfly.

Designed for a slim profile and easy portability, the C28 comes with a stainless steel handle and pocket clip. Chamfered corners along the handle's edge are smooth and rounded to prevent the handle from biting into your palm when pressing down on a hard cut. The C28's blade is flat ground.

Blade Steel	ATS-55
Blade Thickness	3/32in 2.5mm
Clip	Stainless Steel
Diameter of Blade Hole	7/16in 11mm
Edge Type	SpyderEdge
Handle Material	Stainless Steel
Hardness	59-60
Length Blade	2 5/16in 58mm
Length Cutting Edge	1 7/8in 48mm
Length Overall	5 7/16in 138mm
Weight	2.6oz 73g

Production Prototype Pictured

C63 CHINOOK II

Designed by James A. Keating, is of one of Spyderco's largest knives. Designed for the rigors of Martial Blade Craft, and for use as a field, hunting or camp knife. The Chinook II has an upswept modified Bowie-shaped blade, hollow-ground from CPM-S30V steel with a spine swedge. Sandwiched between black G-10 scales, dual liners make the handle and back lock thicker than customary. In so doing the lock is measurably strengthened, bumping it up to an MBC rated strength level and creating one of the strongest locking systems found on any Spyderco model. A deep finger choil and thumb texturing on the blade's spine provide hand purchase for tough cutting. The three screw black metal clip offers left or right handed, tip-up or tip-down carrying positions. The Chinook II is manufactured in Spyderco's Golden, Colorado facility.

Blade Steel	CPM S30V
Blade Thickness	5/32in 4mm
Clip	Stainless steel/black
Diameter of Blade Hole	9/16in 14mm
Edge Type	Plain Edge
Handle Material	G-10
Hardness	59-60
Length Blade	3 3/4in 95mm
Length Closed	4 7/8in 123mm
Length Cutting Edge	3 3/8in 85mm
Length Overall	8 5/8in 219mm
Weight	6 oz (169g)

CIVILIAN

The Civilian was developed for the use of US law enforcement officers. The patented reverse S blade shape evolved to fulfil the back-up needs of undercover agents with little or no training in self-defence. With its paper-thin tip, the Civilian is specifically designed for law enforcement personnel and not designed for general utility or everyday use. The G-10 handle material makes the folder lightweight and a black pocket clip is situated for tip-down pocket carrying. One of the most specialized CLIPITS in the Spyderco line-up, the Civilian is produced in very limited quantities. The blade is hollow-ground.

Blade Steel	ATS-55
Blade Thickness	1/8in 3mm
Diameter of Blade Hole	15/32in 12mm
Edge Type	SpyderEdge
Handle Material	G-10
Hardness	59-60
Length Blade	4 1/8in 105mm
Length Closed	5 3/16in 132mm
Length Cutting Edge	3 3/4in 95mm
Length Overall	9 3/16in 233mm

D'Allara Rescue

D'ALLARA RESCUE

The D'Allara Rescue is named in honour of Officer D'Allara who lost his life in the terrorist attack of 9/11/01.

It is a full-sized Rescue folder with a VG-10 blade and Spyderco's Ball Bearing Lock.

Its contoured and rounded handle has Bi-Directional Texturing and is moulded in black FRN (Fibreglass Reinforced Nylon). It comfortably fills the palm of the hand creating less fatigue while cutting. The fully serrated blade is thick from heel to tip ending in a non-pointed sheep foot. Pulling back on the ball unlocks the blade smoothly and quickly. A wire clip may be attached to either side of the knife to clip the knife to a pocket or strap.

Blade Steel	VG-10
Blade Thickness	1/8in (3mm)
Clip	Heavy-duty wire clip
Diameter of Blade Hole	9/16in 14mm
Edge Type	SpyderEdge
Handle Material	Fibreglass Reinforced Nylon
Hardness	59-60
Length Blade	3 1/2in 88mm
Length Closed	4 15/16in 125mm
Length Cutting Edge	3 3/16in (81mm)
Length Overall	7 7/8in 198mm
Weight	5.75 oz (164g)

DELICA LIGHTWEIGHT

This is a lightweight version of the standard Delica. It has proved very popular and is currently Spyderco's top selling design. Designed to be easily carried for everyday use, the Lightweight is small enough not to raise eyebrows yet big enough for most cutting requirements. The FRN (Fibreglass Reinforced Nylon) handle is fitted with a modified-skinning style blade made of VG-10 stainless steel. It comes in three blade configurations (fully serrated SpyderEdge, plain edge or a 50/50 combination) and is fitted with a black reversible ambidextrous clip.

Blade Steel	VG-10
Blade Thickness	3/32in 2.5mm
Diameter of Blade Hole	15/32in 12mm
Edge Type	50/50, Plain Edge, and SpyderEdge
Handle Material	Fibreglass Reinforced Nylon
Hardness	60-62
Length Blade	3in 77mm
Length Closed	4in 102mm
Length Cutting Edge	2 11/16in 68mm
Length Overall	7in 177mm
Weight	1.9oz 54g

PRODUCTION PROTOTYPE PICTURED

Delica Trainer

DELICA TRAINER

The Delica Trainer is a special unsharpened version of the Delica intended for training and for demonstrations. The FRN handle is fire engine red, identifying it as a non-sharpened Spyderco.

Trainers are identical in size; shape and weight to the standard knife but allow the user to safely practice opening and closing, and retrieval; helping to develop muscle memory. The C11TR Delica Trainer comes equipped with a black metal ambidextrous clip and round contoured, unsharpened blade.

Blade Thickness   3/32" 2.5mm
Clip   Reversible Ambidextrous
Diameter Blade Hole   15/32" 12mm
Edge Type   No Edge
Handle Material   Fibreglass Reinforced Nylon
Hardness   57-58
Length Blade   3" 77mm
Length Closed   4" 102mm
Length Cutting Edge   N/A
Length Overall   9 3/16" 233mm
Weight   2.1oz 38.3g

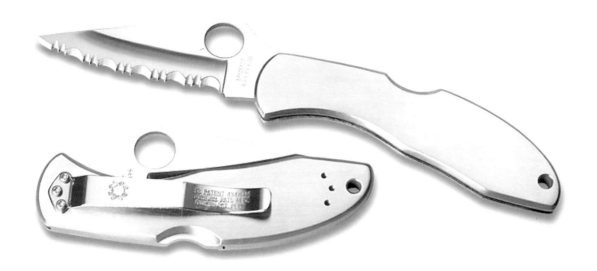

Delica

DELICA

This is the all stainless steel version of Spyderco's popular Delica.

Slightly heavier and more substantial than the lightweight version, it is designed to provide a sense of solidity without being excessively bulky. The smooth metal handle provides a surface area for adding personal engraving or embellishment. The hollow-ground, modified skinning-style blade is made of AUS-6 that has a carbon level of around 1% for advanced edge retention. Two sets of pre-drilled holes allow the clip be positioned for tip-up or tip-down carry.

Blade Steel   AUS-6
Blade Thickness   3/32in 2.5mm
Clip   Stainless Steel, tip-up/tip-down
Diameter of Blade Hole   15/32in 12mm
Edge Type   Plain edge, SpyderEdge
Handle Material   Stainless Steel
Hardness   57-58
Length Blade   2 7/8in 72mm
Length Closed   4in 102mm
Length Cutting Edge   2 1/2in 63mm
Length Overall   6 13/16in 173mm
Weight   4oz 110g

Endura Lightweight

ENDURA LIGHTWEIGHT

This is one of the classic lightweights that form the mainstay of Spyderco's product range. Indeed the Endura model could be said to have started the trend toward lightweight folders. It is very popular as an everyday, general utility, pocket-knife for members of the emergency services.

Blade Steel	VG-10
Blade Thickness	1/8" 3mm
Clip	Reversible Ambidextrous
Diameter of Blade Hole	15/32" 12mm
Edge Type	50/50, plain edge, SpyderEdge
Handle Material	Fibreglass Reinforced Nylon
Hardness	59-60
Length Blade	3 15/16" 100mm
Length Cutting Edge	3 7/16" 87mm
Length Overall	8 13/16" 223mm
Weight	2.9oz 82g

Endura Trainer

ENDURA TRAINER

The Trainer version of the Endura is identical to the standard knife in weight and size but the blade has a dull edge and rounded tip. To identify it as a practice knife the handle is moulded in bright red Fibreglass Reinforced Nylon. It is used as a demonstration knife and to practice opening and closing with one hand, fast retrieval and, martial blade craft moves.

Blade Steel   AUS-6
Blade Thickness   1/8in 3mm
Clip   Reversible Ambidextrous
Diameter Blade Hole   15/32in 12mm
Edge Type   No Edge
Handle Material   Fibreglass Reinforced Nylon
Hardness   58-59
Length Cutting Edge   N/A
Length Overall   8 7/8in 223mm
Weight   3.14oz 89g

Endura

ENDURA

The Endura has been designed as a robust, general-purpose utility knife. It is fitted with a stainless steel handle and is of heavier construction than usual. The handle has flat sides, offering a surface for custom engraving. The C10 Endura has a modified skinning-style, hollow ground blade, laser cut out of AUS-6 high carbon steel. Two sets of pre-drilled holes permit the metal clip to be positioned in a tip-up or tip-down carrying position.

Blade Steel	AUS-6
Blade Thickness	1/8" 3mm
Clip	Stainless Steel, tip-up/tip-down
Diameter of Blade Hole	15/32" 12mm
Edge Type	plain edge, SpyderEdge
Handle Material	Stainless Steel
Hardness	57-58
Length Blade	3 3/4" 96mm
Length Closed	4 13/16" 122mm
Length Cutting Edge	3 1/4" 83mm
Length Overall	8 1/2" 216mm
Weight	5.5oz 156g

Harpy

HARPY

Appropriately named, the blade of the Harpy resembles the claw of an eagle. Designed for controlled, pulling cuts, the Hawksbill blade shape comes from the marine and commercial fishing industries and was developed to enable rope, line, or netting to be cut at arm's length, quickly and effectively. The curved arc of the blade prevents whatever is being cut from slipping off the tip, and is hollow ground. The locking lever is shaped to allow the handle to be gripped tightly without accidentally unlocking the blade. There is a cut out in the stainless steel handle for fast drying when the knife is used in or around water.

Blade Steel	VG-10
Blade Thickness	1/8in 3mm
Clip	Stainless Steel
Diameter of Blade Hole	15/32in 12mm
Edge Type	SpyderEdge
Handle Material	Stainless Steel
Hardness	59-60
Length Blade	2 3/4in 70m
Length Closed	3 7/8in 99mm
Length Overall	6 1/2in 165mm
Weight	3.75oz 106g

MILITARY

Spyderco's Military model is a high performance folder with features designed for heavy-duty use. It is fitted with a black-coated stainless steel blade with a combination plain, serrated edge. This is a modified clip-point pattern, laser cut from CPM-S30V steel and ground flat. Close attention has been paid to the knife's ergonomics which include: a protective finger choil, slip-proof grip where the thumb sits, an oversized opening hole for large or gloved hands and an enlarged handle for a better grip. The Walker LinerLock is recessed into the G-10 hand grip scales, allowing the lock to be strengthened without adding thick or bulky liners. Spacers set between the scales leave the mechanism inside open to view letting accumulated dirt and grime rinse away. The knife is fitted with a three-screw black metal clip, and is carried in a tip-down position.

The Military model is also available with a bright finished blade.

Blade Steel	CPM S30V
Blade Thickness	5/32in 4mm
Clip	Stainless steel/black
Diameter of hole Blade Hole	9/16in 14mm
Edge Type	50/50
Handle Material	G-10
Hardness	59-60
Length Blade	4in 102mm
Length Closed	5 1/2in 139mm
Length Cutting Edge	3 11/16in 93mm
Length Overall	9 1/2in 242mm
Weight	4.2oz 120g

MILITARY

Military G10

C07 POLICE MODEL

The choice of law enforcement officers for over a decade, the C07 is a workhorse. One of the most efficient Spyderco designs to date, the Police Model provides exceptional strength in a slim and comfortable to carry design. Although the Police Model is a big knife it is not too bulky. It's designed to pack as much blade length as possible into a slim handle, little bigger than the blade. The specially designed locking lever allows for a tight grip without accidentally releasing the lock. The C07 is made entirely in stainless steel with a hollow-ground blade in VG-10 stainless steel.

The Police Model is also available with combination plain, serrated edge blade, a black-coated finished and carbon fibre handle.

Blade Steel	VG-10
Blade Thickness	1/8" 3mm
Clip	Stainless Steel
Diameter of Blade Hole	15/32" 12mm
Edge Type	50/50, plain edge, SpyderEdge
Handle Material	Stainless Steel
Hardness	59-60
Length Blade	4 1/8" 104mm
Length Closed	5 5/16" 135mm
Length Cutting Edge	3 13/16" 97mm
Length Overall	9 7/16" 240mm
Weight	5.5oz 155g

Production Prototype Pictured

Rescue 93mm

RESCUE 93MM

The Rescue 93mm has been designed to meet the needs of rescue personnel. It is a readily accessible knife for rapidly cutting a variety of materials, in close proximity to casualties. Spyderco's new C14 Rescue 93mm model was developed from the earlier C14 Spyderco Rescue, the Rescue 93mm has a 3 1/2in cutting edge made from VG-10 stainless steel. The blade is mostly serrated with the last inch at the tip plain edged for a broad range of cutting needs. The blade's tip is a rounded sheepsfoot design (no sharpened point) that slides safely under seatbelts or clothing. A unique feature is the crescent-shaped portion of steel cut from the blade's spine just in front of the hole. While cutting, the crescent provides a positioning spot for the index finger giving perfect control over the blade's tip. Behind the round hole there is a textured thumb grip. Both positioning points are further refined by a finger choil on the underside of the handle where the handle and blade meet. The combined blade and handle shape provide good control and ergonomic comfort for the knife user. Made of fibreglass reinforced nylon resin the handle is indigo blue, textured with a palm grip waffle pattern. A tip-up pocket clip fastens to either side of the handle for both right and left-handed and doubles as a lanyard hole. A cut out in the locking lever (called a David Boye indent) makes the knife impossible to accidentally close when gripped tightly.

Blade Steel   VG-10
Blade Thickness   1/8in 3.2mm
Clip   Stainless Steel
Diameter Blade Hole   9/16in 14.5mm
Edge Type   75/25
Handle Material   Fiberglass Reinforced Nylon
Hardness   59-60
Length Blade   3 5/8in 93mm
Length Closed   4 5/8in 116mm
Length Cutting Edge   3 7/16in 87mm
Length Overall   8 3/16in
Weight   2.6oz 73g

PROTOTYPE PICTURED

Rescue 93mm

Rescue 93mm

Production Prototype Pictured

Salsa

Salsa

The Salsa is the mainstay of Spyderco's line of Little Big Knives, and is designed to be small enough to be used as an everyday pocketknife.

This model introduced the Cobra Hood, a textured thumb rest above the blade hole. The Salsa is available with a black anodized aluminium handle or in a natural-coloured titanium handled version. The Titanium Salsa has an integral compression lock. The aluminium version has the compression lock housed inside the scale. Both models have blades that are flat-ground with the Titanium model's blade made of Hitachi ATS-34 and the Aluminium Salsa made of Aichi AUS-8. A spring-back-tension-wire clip supplied as standard.

Blade Steel	AUS-8
Blade Thickness	3/32" 2.5mm
Clip	Heavy-duty wire clip
Diameter of Blade Hole	9/16" 14mm
Edge Type	plain edge
Handle Material	Anodized Aluminium
Hardness	58-59
Length Blade	2 7/16" 63mm
Length Closed	3 1/2" 89mm
Length Overall	5 5/8" 143mm
Weight	2.5oz 71g

Salsa

Salsa

Production Prototype Pictured

Salt 1

SALT 1

The Salt is based on the design of the Delica model with a few modifications, but it's main difference lies in the choice of materials. The Salt 1 is designed to be used in a salt-water environment and is impervious to rust and pitting. To achieve this the blade is made from H1 steel, manufactured in Japan. H1 steel is a PH steel meaning it is a precipitation-hardened steel. It's naturally hard without heat-treating and with 1% nitrogen instead of carbon it cannot rust. H1 holds a sharpened cutting edge equivalent to many premium carbon steels but without developing rust or pitting. The design of the Salt 1 varies from that of the Delica in a few details. The blade has a rounded tip and its steel components are treated to be impervious to rust and pitting. It has a larger (14mm) opening hole for gloved or wet hands, and the black, fibreglass reinforced nylon handle is textured in a checkerboard pattern. A metal pocket clip attaches for right and left-handed users and there is also a lanyard hole.

Blade Steel	H-1
Blade Thickness	3/32in 2.5mm
Clip	Reversible Ambidextrous
Diameter of Blade Hole	9/16in 14mm
Edge Type	SpyderEdge
Handle Material	Fibreglass Reinforced Nylon
Hardness	57-58
Length Blade	3in 77mm
Length Closed	4in 102mm
Length Cutting Edge	2 11/16in 68mm
Length Overall	7in 177mm
Weight	2oz 56g

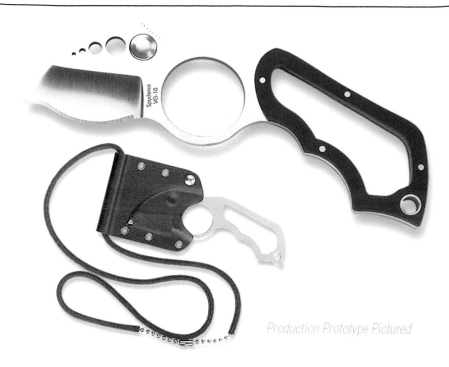

Production Prototype Pictured

S.P.O.T.

S.P.O.T. is an acronym for Self Protection Option Tool and is Spyderco's inaugural offering to the neck knife market.

Designed by Sal Glesser, its shape and size are inspired by the French knife designer Fred Perrin. The S.P.O.T. is a palm-sized all-steel fixed-blade with a skeletally cut out handle. Unique to the model is the index finger hole, a Perrin feature. Placing the index finger through the hole and gripping the angled handle situates the thumb atop the blade's spine for precise cutting control. Curved into a reverse S-shape, the blade is ground to an incisor-like tip for craft projects and other meticulous cutting jobs. A line of graduating-sized holes is drilled out of the blade lessening overall weight. This model is made with VG-10 stainless steel overlaid with Micarta edging along the handle's rim for added grip. Since it's made of one solid piece of stainless steel, the S.P.O.T. has no moving parts to catch, break, or wear-out over time. It is supplied with a lightweight Kydex neck sheath.

Blade Steel	VG-10
Blade Thickness	1/8in 3mm
Case/Sheath	Kydex Sheath
Diameter of Blade Hole	NA
Edge Type	plain edge, SpyderEdge
Handle Material	VG-10 w/Micarta overlay on edging
Hardness	59-60
Length Blade	1 5/8in
Length Closed	NA
Length Cutting Edge	1 3/8in
Length Overall	4 13/16in
Weight	1.3oz (37g)

PROTOTYPE PICTURED

S.P.O.T.

Production Prototype Pictured

S.P.O.T.